Promise

&

Fulfillment

formulas for real bread without gluten

CHRIS STAFFERTON

MILIACEUM

DEVONPORT

First published in Australia in 2019 by
Miliaceum
123 Oldaker Street
Devonport 7310
Australia
www.miliaceum.com

ISBN 978 0 6485549 0 5

10 9 8 7 6 5 4 3

Contents

Acknowledgements

The project of writing a book is almost overwhelming and cannot be done without the support of many people. First and most importantly, my wife Jenny, who has endured the family kitchen being overrun by my bread making activities, equipment, and supplies. All this to produce food that she doesn't need. Together with my daughters; Helen, Laura, and Hannah, as well as my sons-in-law Chris and Jeremy along with many friends, they have been willing and gracious testers of bread designed and baked in our home. Without their honest and demanding critiques, none of the bread would have reached the necessary standard: bread that anyone can enjoy.

This journey began with a determined, but naïve, home cook. Through the gracious responses and engagement of many in the worldwide baking fraternity, both amateur and professional, I have learned much. Special thanks to the members of the BreadChat group hosted on Twitter for many years. Those early morning meet-ups were a special source of learning and engagement with real live bakers. Very special thanks also to Emmanuel Hadjiandreou and François Brault for their encouragement, hospitality and constructive critiques of my work.

I had been milling my own fresh flour for some years before I had the privilege of meeting Paul Lebeau and Wolfgang Mock. When I was searching for my first mill I learned a little about Wolfgang, but I never expected the privilege of getting to know him. I thank them both for their generous encouragement and hospitality.

Still on the international circuit: thanks also to Jarkko Laine and his team at Bread Magazine, and Chris Young and the team at the UK's Campaign for Real Bread. Your focus on real bread, as well as encouraging nurturing the growing bread movement continues to be a source of inspiration and encouragement.

Meeting our own Australian craft baking and milling fraternity in bakeries, and at the GrAiNZ2017 Conference at Dust Bakery in Sydney, and continuing to build relationships since then, has been very important to me. Thank you, Graham, Jay, Ari, Brandon, and Ian, Ces, John, Quentin, Nonie, and many others for the challenges, insights and encouragement I have received.

To Lauren and Henriette Damen at Kindred Organics, thank you for your encouragement and wonderful supplies of organic buckwheat, quinoa and flax.

To those who have bought my recipes online, working with me in sourdough tutorials and the very few local workshops: thank you for the challenging questions and keen interest that spurred me on to learn more and to work at developing this book!

There are many things that can be learned and done by a person with a little time on their hands, but effective editing of words they have written is not one. Thank you to those who have reviewed this book as it has developed, and a special thanks to Gordon for your courteous and courageous challenges to my blinkered vision.

Thank you all!

Then God said, "I give you every seed-bearing plant on the face of the whole earth and every tree that has fruit with seed in it. They will be yours for food."

Genesis 1:29
New International Version (NIV)

A little of my story ...

So how *do* we make bread rise without gluten?

For me, the move to a gluten-free diet was a medical necessity. Developing good bread without gluten became personal: for my own benefit and for the benefit of family members.

When I began this journey baking without gluten I heard many strange comments, suggestions, and statements of strong belief from people who considered themselves to be experts. One of the most curious was: 'you can't make gluten-free bread rise'. This seemed to come from people who had only baked with gluten and they held the opinion that gluten was essential to holding gases in the dough. I have worked as an engineer, a pastor and a chaplain as well as a pest manager in a hydroponic hot-house. In each role, I found an enormous body of knowledge. Within each body of knowledge there was sound knowledge, based on careful observation, investigation and experience. But, in each, there was also dubious 'knowledge' based on guesswork or unanalysed tradition. At best there was little testing of traditions. At worst there was little understanding of the components of bread and how they work together to produce the human invention that has sustained much of the world's civilisations. To be blunt, there were many untested and unsubstantiated claims that misled and misinformed the unwary. So, as I began working to develop good bread without gluten, I approached the task with a sceptical mindset arrived at by experience in a number of fields.

The claim that bread needed gluten to make it work seemed to make sense: gluten is like a plastic or rubber and it holds gas in little bubbles. Or, perhaps not! Perhaps there is more to bread than gluten. Initially, it puzzled me because even with the most basic commercial gluten-free flour mix (white rice flour, tapioca starch and corn starch) I had already been able to prepare leavened bread without gluten. It was not very nice, but it rose with the gases produced by yeast. As I began to read widely and engage humbly with experienced bakers I began to realise that one of the keys to getting a good rise in the dough is using fine flour. With flour that contains plenty of fine, damaged starch particles, it is possible to prepare a dough that will successfully hold a good part of the fermentation gases.

I stumbled across psyllium husk in the early days of my journey with gluten-free bread. My mother-in-law was visiting. Her doctor had put her on a dietary regime that included drinking a cup of hydrated psyllium each morning. I was already working with flax and chia. When I saw the potential of psyllium I began to test some ideas. Before long I was working to see how little psyllium husk I needed to get a beneficial effect in both the dough and the baked bread.

When my work moved into natural fermentation and sourdough I noticed that fewer ingredients were needed. There was something about fermenting with wild yeasts and bacteria that brought out the best in a limited set of ingredients. The interaction of fermentation and fermentation products on the flour and psyllium husk during fermentation did not cause the dough to lose strength. In some cases, the strength of the dough appeared to marginally increase. These observations led me to reduce the set of ingredients in each formula to the minimum possible. My first bread formula with only flour + water + salt + time was Buckwheat Pumpernickel (page 63). Devising techniques to better manage the flour and water led to more styles of bread using a single flour, and a wide range of bread formulas, some of which are featured in this book. As I began to dip into research papers on the microbiology and chemistry of fermentation I learned a little about the processes behind the results I was seeing in my bread. Developing good bread, without gluten, that only uses flour + water + salt + time is an ongoing project.

Chris Stafferton

May 2019

Promise & Fulfilment - real bread without gluten

You may need to know ...

Basic bread, no gluten ...

Baking bread is as old as civilisation. Perhaps it is one of the developments that helped humans adopt a more settled lifestyle. Maybe it was one of the early activities that developed when it was possible to have some basic tools: something to grind seed, something to hold batter or dough until it was baked on stones. It is possible that the earliest breads—flat breads—were made with seeds that have no gluten.[1, 2]

The basics

To make bread, the essential ingredients are flour and water. Salt is for flavour and may have a minor role in the development of the dough, but salt isn't essential. Even amongst breads made from wheat, there are breads that use no salt.

So we could prepare a simple flat bread, without gluten, with no more than flour and water. Ferment some of the flour and it is transformed into a gooey batter. Pour that batter onto a hot stone or skillet and you have a basic bread. Think of *injera*, the bread from Ethiopia made with teff. You can live very well with it! It could be even be promoted as gourmet fare.

Beyond the basics

We all want to eat well. We want to enjoy the aroma, the flavour, the texture and the 'mouthfeel' as well as the appearance. These characteristics all contribute to our enjoyment of food. Then there is the matter of nutrition. When we eat, most of us want to do more than to merely survive; we want to eat to thrive!

Beginning with essentials of flour and water we might add salt and other ingredients. That's where it gets interesting. To decide what to add, we need to know what are we trying to achieve, and what we need to do to get there. We tend to think of bread mainly as risen bread that can be sliced or torn apart to eat with other foods. However, if the bread is particularly good we might prefer to eat it on its own: savouring the flavour, the aroma and the texture of both the crumb and the crust.

So, what do we need to add to get from a flour and water flat bread to a soft, tender crumb and a crisp or a chewy crust? If we were baking with gluten the answer is simple. Nothing else is needed because barley, rye, oats and wheat all have proteins that provide at least a basic 'matrix' (the technical term for the bread's structure) that helps the dough to contain gases, mainly carbon dioxide, produced by fermenting flour. When we are working with other flours without those proteins the matrix is not so easy to produce.

It is common practice to add a binder or gum to provide a matrix for the dough. Some of these additives are natural ingredients, others are industrial products prepared by fermentation. Whatever their origin most of the additives function as a hydrocolloid. When the hydrocolloid is worked into the dough it helps to develop a matrix that retains fermentation gases. Most of the additives contain oligosaccharides and polysaccharides. All are approved by various government agencies for human consumption. If you take a slow walk down a supermarket aisle, examining the ingredients labels on food packages and you will find most of the oligosaccharide and polysaccharide-based ingredients in many foods. Often they have 'E' numbers for additives, and are listed as thickeners, emulsifiers or stabilisers. Some of these additives are beginning to have reputations as allergens or potential allergens. So, we need to choose wisely, and be careful not to overuse any of these additives.

Many of the formulas in this book use psyllium husk or psyllium husk powder to develop the dough matrix. Psyllium husk is the seed coat of the plantago plant. I like it because it is effective in helping to provide structure to the dough and it doesn't modify the flavour of the dough. It adds dietary fibre to the bread and may have a number of health benefits like lowering cholesterol.[3] Care should be taken not to over-use psyllium husk or any other dietary fibre,[4]

We now have a good set of essential ingredients to prepare bread: flour, water, salt and a hydrocolloid to help with structure. With this group of essential ingredients, it is possible to make a wide range of breads. The style and quality of the bread we produce with these ingredients will depend on:

- the quality of the ingredients
- the quantity of each ingredient
- the time taken
- the skills and techniques applied

1   Jeremy Cherfas. Millet: How A Trendy Ancient Grain Turned Nomads Into Farmers, NPR, December 23, 2015. https://n.pr/2FJ7YbB
2   Dan Saladino talks to Modernist Bread author, Nathan Myhrvold. The Future of Bread https://bbc.in/2uFCZrU

3   Sprecher D.L., Harris B.V., Goldberg A.C., Anderson E.C., Bayuk L.M., Russell B.S., et al. Efficacy of Psyllium in Reducing Serum Cholesterol Levels in Hypercholesterolemic Patients on High- or Low-Fat Diets. *Ann Intern Med.* October 1, (1993) https://bit.ly/2TTmvGK (accessed 22Apr, 2019)
4   James S. L., Muir J. G. , Curtis S. L. , and Gibson P. R. . Clinical Perspectives - Dietary fibre: a roughage guide. *Internal Medicine Journal* (2003); 33. https://rdcu.be/buroU (accessed 22Apr, 2019)

Using this book and formulas in this book

The **first section** of this book provides background information that may be helpful as you grapple with preparing to bake using the bread formulas (that is, the recipes) in the rest of the book. This section covers the process of baking bread, from preparing to bake to cooling the bread.

There are **10 sections of bread formulas** with formulas grouped according to common characteristics.

Finally, there is a **Resources section** that provides a 'Summary of Key Ingredients' and a 'Free From...' advice table that indicates if known allergens are used in a bread formula. There is also a guide to troubleshooting problems, and glossary of terms used in the book.

Each bread formula is provided on a two-page spread. The left page displays the photograph of the bread, the right page provides most of the information required to prepare the bread.

In the top right hand corner of each formula is a summary key that indicates the following information: What it makes, what needs to be milled (if you are milling your own flour), how long from start to finish, the baking time, and the leaven. Where a bread pan is required the size of the pan is also indicated in the summary.

Below the summary is a schedule that takes you from the preparation of the leaven, to cooling the bread.

Following down the column, on most pages there are list of ingredients.

On the body of the page you will find the method for each bread. Each formula follows the process for making dough and baking bread. With a few formulas the method begins below the photograph on the left page and extends to fill the right page.

Some formulas include a variation, usually for a different leaven.

Millet & Buckwheat Cottage Loaf

There is little as satisfying as a good rustic loaf. The Millet & Buckwheat loaf is a wholesome bread, full of flavour and the romance of a traditional country bread.

This can be made as with a sourdough starter, or with a yeast-based preferment.

Summary
Makes: 1 loaf x 1050g

Milling: buckwheat, millet, chia, flax

Time to prepare: 20 hours

Baking time: 50 minutes

Leaven: millet leaven or baker's yeast

Activity	Time	Total
Preparing leaven	0:05	0:05
Fermenting leaven	8:00	8:05
Building dough	0:10	8:15
Fermenting	8:00	16:15
Shaping	0:05	16:20
Proving	2:00	18:20
Baking	0:50	19:10
Cooling	1:00	20:10

Leaven
Mix 20g millet starter with 40g water and 45g millet flour.

Cover the bowl or jug and allow the mixture to ferment for around eight hours.

Dough
In a large mixing bowl combine all the dry ingredients: 180g millet flour, 180g buckwheat flour, 50g chia meal, 30g flax meal, 10g psyllium husk, and 3g salt.

Gently with a whisk to ensure there are no lumps of chia and flax meal.

Mix 450g tepid water and 30g honey with the leaven.

Pour the leaven mixture onto the dry ingredients and combine well.

Fermenting
Cover the dough and set the dough to rise for 8 hours in a warm place.

Shaping
Dust the kneading board lightly and gently knead the dough by stretching and folding it.

Divide the dough into two lumps, one roughly 750g and 250g.

Shape dough into two balls.

Place the larger ball on a baking sheet, then place the smaller ball on the top centre of the larger ball.

Using a thumb press down through the middle of both balls to form the 'cottage'.

Proving
Cover shaped dough.

Set dough to rise for 2 hours in a warm, draft free place.

Preheat the oven to 220°C.

The loaf can be scored just before baking, if desired.

Baking
Bake in a hot oven (210°C) for 50 minutes.

Cooling
Remove the loaf from the oven and place on a rack to cool.

Variation
This variation allows the Millet & Buckwheat Cottage Loaf to be leavened with baker's yeast, either instant yeast or fresh yeast.

Leaven
1g	instant yeast
(2g)	(fresh yeast)
45g	water
60g	fine millet flour

Leaven
20g	millet starter
40g	water
45g	fine millet flour

Dough
105g	leaven
180g	millet flour
180g	buckwheat flour
50g	chia seeds (meal)
30g	flax seeds (meal)
10g	psyllium husks
3g	salt
30g	honey
450g	tepid water

Additional buckwheat flour for dusting the workbench and the proving basket.

Mastering the process of making bread

Before we begin to assemble and combine ingredients, we need to decide what sort of bread we want to make. That decision will help us to choose the ingredients to use and the techniques that will help us to prepare and manage the ingredients to produce the bread we want. This is not merely about following a formula. It requires a clear understanding of the bread-making process.

The basic process for making dough and baking bread is as follows.

1. preparing to bake
2. building dough
3. fermenting dough
4. shaping dough
5. proving dough
6. baking dough
7. cooling bread

By varying times, temperatures, and techniques, we can adapt this general process to develop different styles of bread.

Adjustments that can be made at each of the steps may include:

- adding desired ingredients
- increasing or reducing the quantity of an ingredient
- extending or reducing the time
- increasing or reducing the temperature
- working the dough more, or less
- using manual or mixing and kneading, or using mechanical mixing or kneading
- managing the humidity during fermentation or baking, and
- managing the process of cooling the bread. This may include applying a glaze

Each of the formulas in this book is structured with the general process in mind. Each formula has adapted the general process with the aim of getting the best from the ingredients and the techniques.

1.   Preparing to bake

This step is where the main decisions are made, since the choices made at this point will determine the overall result of the bake.

First, we assemble our implements and our ingredients. We may choose to buy pre-milled flour, or to mill the flour ourselves. We may need to prepare some of the ingredients, like leaven or malt, ahead of time.

For the leaven we may use bakers' yeast, a sourdough starter, yeast water, or some other liquid leaven. Our preparations might include culturing and preparing the starter. It may be a simple liquid leaven, or it may be a more complex starter built and modified in stages like a *pasta madre* or *lievito madre*. We may choose to use water kefir or milk kefir or prepare a yeast water, or a bee barm.

If our bread is to be flavoured or enriched, we might toast or soak seeds, add spices, steep dried fruit or vegetables, or prepare a paste made from fruit, vegetables or nuts to incorporate in the dough. We might enrich our dough with fats, sugars, liquids or eggs. Each of these additional ingredients will add character and flavour to the dough. Some of them work together to express a particularly rich characteristic, like butter and eggs in brioche. Some ingredients, when added in a particular way, provide striking characteristic breads like brioche and other viennoiserie.

We need to choose a form of hydrocolloid that will assist in providing structure to the dough. This may be psyllium husk, chia seed or flax seed, or some other seed that provides a gel in the dough matrix. To achieve the same effect as psyllium we need 5 grams of chia meal or 6 grams of flax meal. If we use flax or chia, we must be aware that their flavours may dominate the final dough. While it is possible to develop a lighter dough using psyllium than is possible using flax or chia, psyllium does not provide the level of nutrients available from chia or flax. The choice of flax, chia or psyllium depends on what sort of bread is being made.

Our choice of leaven may influence the amount of added hydrocolloid. Some leavens are rich in exopolysaccharides (EPS) produced by the lactic acid bacteria and other bacteria in the microbiome of the leaven. EPS are another form of hydrocolloid that can provide some structure in the dough. A leaven rich in EPS may reduce or eliminate the need for hydrocolloids to be added to the dough.

We may require liquids for dipping dough, or seeds and spices for dressing the dough. We may need egg, milk, butter, sugar, honey, or a glaze for finishing the dough.

We need to assemble all implements and equipment required for the bread we are preparing.

2.   Building dough

With the equipment and ingredients assembled, and with the leaven prepared we can begin combining the ingredients. We might do this in one stage or in multiple stages. We might first build the dough as a pre-ferment, then as a complete dough. We might prepare a number of components of the dough in stages to bring together in a final dough. Using multiple builds and stages allows us to manage the activity, flavour, and structure of the dough.

The essential part of making dough is getting moisture into the flour and its starches. Usually water is used to hydrate the dough. To assist of improve hydration[1] we might also include techniques like *autolysis* (described by Raymond Calvel in *The Taste of Bread*[2]) or *bassinage* for ensuring that the flour has absorbed as much of the liquid as possible, and to enhance flavours and the structure of the dough. We might scald some flour. We might add a soaker of seeds or fruits. We might prepare an enrichment, or simply use warmer water in the dough.

An important part of the building process is mixing or kneading the dough. We might simply mix the dough, or we might work the dough a more intentionally. We might work the dough by hand, squeezing, spreading, and stretching, rolling and folding it to work the liquid thoroughly into the flour. If the dough is very soft, we might simply stretch or spread it slightly and fold it over onto itself. We might choose to knead dough mechanically using stand mixer and dough hook. We might decide to knead only by hand. Kneading the dough well during this stage of the baking process is important for making sure all the ingredients, especially the liquids, are thoroughly incorporated into the dough.

3.   Fermenting dough

At some stage the dough needs to be left alone to do its own thing. The microbes that have been included in the dough need time to do their work. The food for the microbes has already been determined. The main technique we use at this stage is adjusting the temperature. We might already have built a warm dough, or we might have built a cool the dough. Now we can place the dough in a warmer or a cooler place to ferment. By adjusting the temperature, we might increase the activity of some microbes and reduce the activity of others. This allows us to modify the fermentation products and the flavours. Depending on the temperature we might also adjust the time allowed for fermentation at this stage of the process. A long cool ferment will enhance the flavours, a short, warm ferment will produce a milder bread more quickly.

1   See notes on hydraton on page 44.
2   Calvel, Raymond, Ronald L. Writs, James J. MacGuire. The Taste of Bread. New York: Springer Science+Business Media, 2001.

4.   Shaping dough

Shaping the dough might be as simple as forming the dough into a desired shape like a stick, or a bun, or a batard, or a boule. During shaping we might add fruit, nuts, spices, or fillings to the dough. At this stage in the life of the dough these additional ingredients are usually spread on the dough and then folded all rolled into the dough to form the final shape. We might add fat to the dough as we laminate to make croissants or other *viennoiserie*. If we are laminating the dough, we will also need to manage the temperature of the dough and the fat.

The approach we take to shaping will depend on the character of the dough. With a delicate dough that readily cracks, the dough is worked carefully into a log or ball shape, according to the proving basket that will be used. If the dough is more robust, elastic and extensible, the dough can be worked into a log or a ball by first spreading the dough, then rolling it and progressively, but gently, tightening the outer skin of the dough to create a little surface tension in the skin.

The strength of the dough will determine the size and shape produced. Most free form doughs perform best if the cross-section is no more than 9cm when it is shaped. Some doughs are quite delicate and need to be shaped to a smaller cross-section of between 3cm and 5cm. Some sourdoughs, like the dough for Amaranth baguettes, will collapse if they are made into large shapes.

5.   Proving dough

The final fermentation of the dough, where the microbes complete their work producing flavour and shape, is often called 'proving' or 'proofing'. Just like the earlier fermentation, we might adjust the time, temperature and humidity of the dough to produce the bread we want. Proving at a higher temperature will prepare the dough more quickly and produce fewer sour notes in the baked bread. Cold-proving, can be used to extend the final fermentation and produces more complex flavours in the final loaf.

Using a proving basket (banneton) or a cloth (or *couche*) to hold the dough during proving is part of the process for developing the thicker, chewy crust by drying the surface of the dough. The stronger dough skin helps the dough retain its shape when it is being baked. Proving dough in a loaf pan provides a thinner, softer crust.

The time allowed for proving varies from bread to bread. It takes time to learn when the dough has proved. There are a few techniques that can be useful as guides:

•   the dough has doubled in volume (remember that double volume is not the same as double length, width and height, double volume[3])

•   the dough feels soft and tender to the touch when caressed (this is very subjective measure that takes practice to appreciate).

3   See notes about dough volume on page 46.

6.   Baking dough

During baking there are techniques that can be used to adjust and manage the quality of the final bread. The three variables we normally adjust during baking are time, temperature, and humidity. Our choice of techniques will depend on the style of bread being made, the ingredients in the dough and the capabilities of the oven.

The position the dough is placed in an oven will influence the success of the bake. The top shelf of a domestic oven is usually the hottest place. This is where breads with a crisp crust are baked, as well as those that are baked quickly. The middle of the oven works well for pan loaves and larger loaves that take longer to bake. Using the middle of the oven reduces the likelihood of a burned top crust. For long slow baking the middle to lower part of the oven are used. If the oven has a heating element in the base, the lower part should be avoided, or a heavy baking sheet placed on a shelf low in the oven can be used to moderate the radiant heat reaching the base of the loaf.

A baking stone may be used to adjust the transmission of heat to the dough. Baking stones enable us to use radiant heat, not just convective heat to cook the dough. The thicker the stone, the more heat it can store. Preheating the oven will take longer if a baking stone is used. A ceramic pizza stone can be quite durable. Terracotta tiles are less durable and should only be used if they are certified contaminant-free.

Steam enhances development of the crust, and the development of the crumb inside. Steam can be introduced in to the oven in a number of ways. Common methods are:

*   a dish of water placed low in the oven

*   water misted into the oven when the dough is placed in the oven

*   the surface of the dough misted just prior to the dough being placed in the oven

We might also make use of moisture from the dough, without introducing extra steam to the oven, by using a ceramic, pressed metal, or cast iron cloche to enclose the dough and confine the steam from the baking dough. A light weight cloche will conserve much of the steam from the baking loaf. A heavy duty ceramic or cast iron cloche will also provide radiant heat around the loaf. A purpose designed cloche can be bought, or there are a number of items of common bake ware items that can be re-purposed to use as a cloche. These include:

*   a 'Dutch Oven', either cast iron or ceramic (care should be taken when handling these especially if they are preheated before the dough is placed in them, as well as when the lid is removed and when the loaf is removed)

*   a lidded baking dish (these may be pressed metal, cast iron or clay/ ceramic)

If we are making pretzels or bagels they are dipped in a boiling bath before baking. This gelatinizes the crust of the pretzel or bagel before baking and helps to retain moisture and gas in the crumb.

If we are making doughnuts or flatbread wraps, we won't use an oven! Doughnuts are cooked in an oil bath and wraps can be very effectively cooked in a sandwich press.

Cutting, slashing, or scoring the skin of the dough allows the dough to expand in the oven in a more controlled manner. As the dough warms final gas production occurs and gas and moisture in dough expand causing the dough to rise. This expansion is referred to as 'oven spring'. If oven spring is not controlled the dough will expand and break through weak spots in the dough skin. The scoring pattern in the upper skin of the dough can harness oven spring and encourage vertical rise of the dough. If the sides of the dough are scored, those scores can allow horizonal 'rise', resulting in a loaf that looks a bit like a pancake.

As the dough cooks, gases already in the dough from fermentation and steam from the moisture in the dough expand forming the alveoli, or gas bubbles in the bread. As the dough heats and the alveoli form the starches in the dough gelatinize, forming an open structure in the dough. As the dough reaches the limit of its ability to stretch the bubbles burst. If the starches have gelatinized[4] and set sufficiently the dough will retain the structure, even when the alveoli burst. If the starches have begun to gelatinize, but have not set when the alveoli burst, the dough will begin to collapse.

As a rule of thumb the dough should be baked when the internal temperature of the dough is about 96 degrees Celsius to 97 degrees Celsius. A probe thermometer is used to check the internal temperature of the loaf. Be as quick as you can checking the loaf temperature. If possible, keep the loaf in the oven while the temperature is checked. If the loaf has not yet reached the temperature continue baking for at least another 10 minutes (10 minutes allows the oven to reach the baking temperature after heat has been lost when the oven is opened).

7.   Cooling bread

When it comes to cooling the bread, we must think about the sort of bread we are baking and the best way to cool the bread before it is served. Some breads, like focaccia or pizza require very little or no cooling. Other breads, like pumpernickel, need to be cooled slowly and rested for at least 24 hours before they cut and served. When bread is cooling, it is also drying as excess moisture escapes from the baked dough. For very delicate doughs, like panettone, we hang the loaf upside down to prevent the delicate crumb from collapsing as it cools and dries. With some breads, like the 'Homage to Borodinski' (page 101), we return the loaf to a cooling oven for a short time. This allows the bread to shed moisture and the crust hardens slightly.

---

4   See notes on gelatinization on page 47.

Flours

Although gluten-free flours can be bought ready milled in pre-mixes, I prefer not to use pre-mixes. First, I like to be sure that I am keeping a varied and balanced diet. I don't want to return to over-consuming one flour. There are many useful and nutritious flours available, so why focus on just one or two? I also like to know what contribution an individual flour is making to the dough and the final bread. I also like to know that my ingredients are fresh. Pre-mixes that have a longer shelf life are generally prepared from refined, processed starches sometimes extracted from whole flours. If the germ is included, the flour does not keep well and tends to become rancid. So, pre-milled flour may have the germ and other nutrients removed. This means, unfortunately, that refined flours with a long shelf life generally have lower nutritional value and less flavour.

Whole grain vs refined

With pre-milled flour, it is never clear if the flour has been sifted to extract any part of the flour. As sifting is the accepted practice with wheaten flours, it is probably fair to expect that the same is happening with gluten-free flours. The fine quality of most pre-milled gluten-free flours combined with the long shelf life suggests some refinement or modification to the flour.

Freshly milled vs pre-milled

For flavour and performance, both in bread starter culture and in the dough, freshly milled flour is better than pre-milled flour. Buying pre-milled flour has a few drawbacks:

- wholegrain or whole-seed flour begins to deteriorate as soon as it is milled,

- older flour is more likely to have a bitter taste or aftertaste: this indicates the natural oils in the flour, from the seed, have become rancid,

- where pre-milled flour does not become rancid it is likely that it is not wholegrain: parts of the flour have already been removed.

The freshest flour you can get is the flour you mill just before you use it. Your own freshly milled flour has all the components of the seed, all the natural oils, as well as all the minerals, starches, and enzymes are in the flour. They are all are ready for you to make the best use of them.

A ready reference finding which flours are used in bread formulas is provided in the Key Ingredient Charts on pages 190 - 193.

Amaranth

Flavour: Mildly sweet with a slight nuttiness and earthiness.

Use: Amaranth flour works well as a low percentage of the total flour. It can be mixed with starches or other whole flours

Issues: Amaranth can become stale and rancid if pre-milled and stored for long periods.

Being a small seed, amaranth has a low starch and a higher level of seed coat and minerals. So mixing it with higher starch flours, or with starches, can help form a tasty and nutritious dough.

Buckwheat

Flavour: Good buckwheat has a slightly sweet, grassy flavour with earthy notes.

Use: Buckwheat flour can be used for up to 100% of the flour in the dough. Cracked groats or toasted groats can be used in dough. Toasted or roasted groats can be milled to flour and added as a proportion of the flour in a dough. Buckwheat can be malted to produce a diastatic malt flour that is high in enzyme activity[1]. It can be also used to produce toasted malt powders used for flavouring and colouring, A liquid malt that is higher in sugars can also be produced by mixing buckwheat flour, diastatic malt, and toasted malt powders (see page 43).

Buckwheat flour can be used to prepare a very useful starter culture.

Issues: Buckwheat that is excessively earthy, bitter, and musty may have been spoiled during transport and storage.

Chestnut

Flavour: Chestnut flour has a sweet, nutty flavour.

Use: Chestnut flour can be used as a thickener. I find it works well paired with buckwheat at a rate of 1part chestnut flour to 3 parts buckwheat flour.

Issues: Chestnut flour is not always readily available, and it is an expensive flour. I prepare my own by collecting or buying chestnuts when they are fresh, in season. If you are collecting them, remove the spiny husk. Score the shell of the nut then bake at 170 degrees Celsius. As the shells open remove the chestnuts from the oven and allow them to cool until they can be handled. Peel the shells from the kernels. Crumble the kernels then dry the kernels. The cooling oven can be used to dry the crumbled kernels. Be sure to crumble

---

1   See pages 42 & 43 forinformation on malting and roasting seed. The temperatures and times for toasting malted buckwheat seed acan also be used for toasting buckwheat seed.

the kernels as small as possible. When the crumbles are dry and hard remove from the oven and allow them to cool. Then allow them to stand for up to 24 hours before milling to a fine flour. Store the flour in an airtight container in a freezer.

Millet (proso)

Flavour: The formulas in this book use proso millet (*Panicum miliaceum*). It has mild, almost wheat-like flavours with a sharpness that increases as the flour ages. Finely milled, freshly milled millet adds mild flavours to the dough.

Use: Millet can be used for up to 100% of the flour in a dough, but generally it is better at anywhere between 50% to 70% of the flour in a dough that includes buckwheat flour, tapioca starch, or a rice flour. Millet can be malted to produce a diastatic malt flour that is high in enzyme activity, or it can be used to produce a liquid malt that is higher in sugars.

Issues: There are many different millets and their characteristics vary. Some millets (pearl millet and fonio millet in particular) have been found to have anti-thyroid properties. Fermentation of millets is said to reduce or remove the problem. If you have thyroid problems, check with your dietitian or health specialist before using millets regularly in your diet. Pre-milled millet flour is often too coarse to use in large proportions in a dough. Pre-milled millet can often have a sharp, bitter aftertaste.

Quinoa

Flavour: Quinoa has a rich nutty, slightly earthy flavour.

Use: Quinoa is a good flour that can be used in many different types of bread. Quinoa makes the most robust and effective sourdough starter. It is active, robust, and resilient.

Issues: The raw, untreated seed has a coating of saponin that protects the seed in the field from bird and insect attack. This may cause the flour to have a sharp or bitter after taste if the saponin-rich seed coating has not been completely removed. The coating must be removed by either triple washing or mechanical polishing. Seed may be bought with the saponin coat removed by either washing or polishing. Washing the seed is a simple process using a fine mesh colander or sieve. The seed should be dried quickly and thoroughly before storage or milling. Seed can be dried in a very cool oven, or using a food dehydrator set to about 45 degrees Celsius. When dry the washed seed can be stored in an airtight container until it is milled.

Quinoa flour is usually available as a creamy-white flour. Seed is usually available as a white or ivory coloured seed. Sometimes red and black seed varieties can be bought. The coloured varieties also mill well and can provide an interesting variation in a loaf.

Rice

Flavour: Whole grain rice has more flavour than polished rice. Many flavours are available with the many varieties available that can be milled. Flavours range from mild, slightly grassy, through nutty flavours to smoky flavours.

Use: Rice can be used for up to 100% of the flour in a dough, or it can be mixed with other flours or starches.

Issues: Rice flour that is pre-milled tends to be either brown or white, although sometimes black rice is available. White rice flour is usually either medium to long grain rice or sweet rice. Most pre-milled rice has a mild or bland flavour. If rice flour is bitter, it is either old or has not been kept well.

Rice, like most seeds, has two types of starch: amylose and amylopectin. As a rule of thumb, the longer and thinner the rice grains the higher the proportion of amylose and lower the proportion of amylopectin. Shorter grain rice tends to be waxy or sticky when cooked, due to the higher levels of amylopectin in those varieties. These include arborio rice, sushi rice and sweet or sticky rice. Most gluten-free bread flours made with medium-grain rice work well as medium-grain rice has a good balance of the two starches.

White rice or polished rice has had the seed coat and bran removed, so the nutrient content is lower than unpolished black, red, purple or brown rice.

Arborio rice mills to a soft, creamy flour that can be used to make delicate doughs, especially when used with flour from the harder longer grain rice or millet.

Red rice is less common. It is very hard rice, and even when milled on the finest settings gives a coarser flour.

Long grain black rice has a rich, slightly smoky aroma. It has a more substantial husk, this gives a slightly coarser flour, even on the finest settings. Black rice flour requires higher hydration; however, it also seems to release the water more quickly.

Flour made from sweet or sticky black rice can be used with other flours to build a good, workable dough, however, sweet rice flour should usually not exceed 40% of the flour.

Sorghum

Flavour: Sorghum, like proso millet, has mild almost wheat like flavours. White sorghum has milder flavours than red sorghum.

Use: Sorghum can be used for up to 100% of the flour in the dough. It also works well at anywhere between 50% and 70% of a dough that includes buckwheat flour, tapioca starch or a rice flour.

Issues: It has a higher starch content than millet and a good balance of amylose and amylopectin.

Sorghum can be malted, but there is a risk of cyanide poisoning.[2] Careful processing of the sprouted seeds can reduce the risk.

Teff

Flavour: Teff is a very small seed with a rich, slightly sweet, nutty flavour. Brown teff has a slightly stronger flavour than ivory teff.

Uses: Teff works well with many other gluten-free flours, especially buckwheat and quinoa. Teff can be used for up to 100% of the flour in the dough.

Issues: Being such small seed teff has a high mineral to starch ratio and it has high levels of nutrients. Teff is usually available in ivory and brown forms: the brown form is higher in iron than the ivory form. Teff can be used to make a very effective starter culture which is higher in strains of the common yeast *Saccharomyces cerevisiae*.[3]

Toasted flours

To increase the intensity of flavour seed can be toasted before milling. This imparts a 'nutty' flavour to the flours. Seed should be toasted at about 170 degrees Celsius. The

2   Traditional processing methods
https://bit.ly/2CRGaRT
The complete book: Lubin, David. Sorghum and Millets in Human Nutrition. FAO, Rome. (1995)
https://bit.ly/2XeDvdu (accessed 22 APR, 2019)

3   Moroni, Alice V., Arendt, Elke K., Fabio Dal Bello. Biodiversity of lactic acid bacteria and yeasts in spontaneously-fermented buckwheat and teff sourdoughs. *Food Microbiology* 28 (2011)
https://bit.ly/2UjFHlx (accessed 22 APR, 2019)

time they are toasted will determine the strength of colour and the intensity of flavour. The longer seeds are toasted the darker and more intense the flavours become. Toasted seed should be allowed to cool before it is milled.

Starches

Adding starches like tapioca and sweet potato starch (as well as arrowroot, cornstarch, potato starch and other vegetable derived starches) can be very useful as they provide very fine particles to the flour that can improve the dough. This is especially the case for doughs made with coarser wholegrain flours, where these starches can provide an inexpensive way to add fine flour particles that allow the dough to hold together better. In my early years of making bread without gluten, I found that around 50% starch in a dough could provide a light, and open crumb if made properly.[4] Most starches are interchangeable in formulas, although some root-based flours like taro flour and cassava flour provide more fibre than the starches prepared from the same type of roots.

4   This was very helpful when one of my children was on a severely limited diet. By using starches, and without a flour mill, I was able to develop many of my earlier formulas including Honey Pumpkin Rolls (page 129) using a minimum of ingredients.

Tools

If you don't have a fully equipped kitchen or if you are starting out, take your time and don't spend too much on tools. There are only a few essentials:

- *somewhere to store a little flour*
- *somewhere to prepare dough*
- *somewhere to bake bread*
- *something to prevent the dough from drying out too quickly*
- *If you are preparing sourdough a few clean, recycled jars or food safe containers will be useful (not metallic as sourdough starters produce mild acids)*

The most important tools are the skills you will develop through preparing and handling dough. Observe, take notes. On page 39 you will find a sheet designed for recording most of the details of a bake. With experience, you will find the information that helps you most.

Here is a list of the tools I use:

1.   Hands

Clean hands are a great asset and they are so useful for many activities in the bakery. They can be used for mixing dough, moving dough, and shaping dough. They are very useful for checking the temperature of warm doughs (around body temperature) or cool doughs.

2.   Oven

This may seem a little obvious, but a few comments are needed. Every oven is different. Get to know your oven. There will be idiosyncrasies, there are in every oven. Ovens often develop problems as they get old. Some ovens have hot-spots, or they have cooler areas. Even a fan-forced oven may not heat all areas consistently. Oven door seals deteriorate as they get old and they can begin to leak heat and steam from the oven. As a thermostat gets older it can become less reliable and may appear to be a little erratic.

3.   Oven thermometer

This is the most overlooked piece of equipment, but one of the most important. Manufacturers of some home ovens allow a variation of 10% from the indicated temperature. That can mean a difference of 20 degrees Celsius — enough to burn a loaf or leave it under-baked. An oven thermometer will help you to understand what the oven is doing as the thermostat operates. An oven thermometer will help you answer these questions:

- Is the oven working at the temperature indicated?

- Does the thermostat regulate the temperate quickly, or does it respond slowly?
- How quickly does it take to reach the temperature?
- How quickly does it return to the temperature?

4.   Workbench

This can be a bit personal: how much space do you have? How much space do you require? I have prepared bread in tiny spaces as well as much more generous spaces.

5.   Digital Scales

Yes, you can live without these, but they make life so much easier. It is easy to get the dough the right consistency if you are able to use accurate scales to weigh quantities of flour, water and other ingredients. Most digital scales made home kitchens, measure in both metric and traditional units.

6.   Timer

The timing of making bread can be quite relaxed during the early stages, particularly with long fermented bread. However, the closer to baking we move, and especially during the bake, the more we need to take notice of timing. There is nothing more disheartening than a kitchen full of acrid smoke when we had anticipated the aroma of fresh bread to fill the kitchen and tantalise the neighbourhood. An inexpensive kitchen timer is good, but in these days of smartphones, we have a suitable tool at our fingertips!

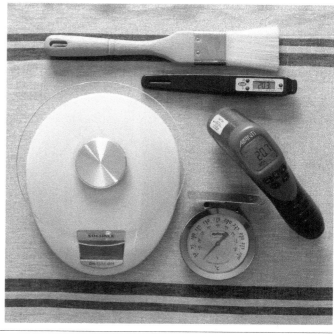

7. Mixing bowls

You may prefer to mix all the ingredients on the workbench. However, mixing bowls are also useful for measuring and preparing to mix ingredients.

8. Dough scrapers

A few inexpensive dough scrapers made from polypropylene or some other food-safe plastic and metal dough scrapers are useful for working on the bench, as well as scraping dough from bowls and other containers.

9. Rolling Pins

A smooth, well balanced rolling pin is essential for laminating dough for croissants and brioche *feuilettée*. Rice & chia wraps, pizza dough and crispbreads are other breads where a good rolling pin will be required.

10. Cloths

Traditionally, in gluten baking, linen cloth is the best option. Baking without gluten has the advantage that the dough seldom sticks, so cotton cloths are suitable with gluten-free baking. Choose good quality, sturdy, closely woven cloth rather than fluffy, loosely woven cloth.

11. Butter muslin

A small sheet of butter muslin (30cm x 30cm) is used for wrapping *lievito madre*. Butter muslin can also be used as a liner for preventing sticky dough from adhering to the proving basket.

12. *Couche*

Couche is one of those wonderful French words that has so many meanings and shade of meaning. Here it is a heavy-duty cloth made from linen. It is used to hold and cover the dough during its final proving, before baking. The couche may be lightly or heavily dusted with flour. As moisture from the skin of the dough is absorbed by the *couche* the skin strengthens and provides structure to the free form loaf. Begin by using a large, clean, closely woven tea towel or dish drying cloth.

13. Cooling Rack

Preferably metal, preferably stainless steel.

14. Proving basket/ banneton

There are so many ways to describe this and so many simple things to use as containers for proving bread. A basket or bowl, often lined with cloth, can be used to assist in producing a desired shape with the dough. It is possible to buy expensive or inexpensive bannetons online. However, a cloth-lined mixing bowl, colander, or polypropylene bread basket will perform the same function: holding the shape of the proving dough and drying the skin of the dough.

15. Baking sheet

A baking sheet is useful for baking free form loaves, or rolls and buns. It can be used as a peel if you are using a baking stone. A baking sheet should be lightly dusted before the dough is placed on it.

16. Baking Pans

When we want a fixed, repeatable shape of bread, especially for sliced sandwiches or toast, a loaf pan is a useful tool. They come in a range of sizes that often relate to the weight of a commercial bread size and weight. For gluten-free pan loaves in this book there are two recommended sizes: 17cm x 10cm x 10cm and 23cm x 10cm x 10cm. Both pans provide deep loaves. For baguettes, 2 or 3 baguette pans are available.

17. Peel

Either a wooden or metal peel for moving dough from the workbench to the baking stone. A pizza peel is ok, or a cookie sheet that has a straight edge without a lip or side to it. A piece of plywood sanded to a smooth finish and oiled lightly with olive oil or some light cooking oil is also suitable. If you are baking baguettes and prefer not to use a baguette pan, a few long plywood peels will be useful.

18. A *lame* or scoring knife

A *lame* is a razor-sharp blade used for scoring or slashing the top of a loaf to control the expansion of the dough in the oven. Not all loaves are scored. For many gluten-free loaves, a sharp paring knife or a fruit knife is enough to score the dough. However, a *lame* can give a cleaner and more precise cut.

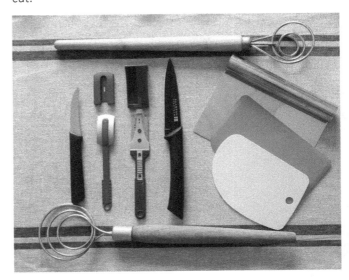

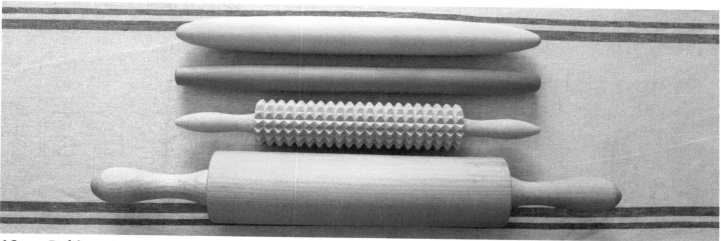

19. Baking stone

A baking stone works by absorbing heat that is transferred to the dough as radiant heat during baking. In general, the larger the stone the better, however, a bigger stone requires longer preheating, so it is more expensive to use. If you are looking at natural stone, it should be free from defects as defects will become hot-spots and may cause the stone to fracture or spall. Unglazed terracotta floor tiles are useful, inexpensive, but also short lived. For a home oven, ceramic pizza stones are inexpensive and durable stones. They have been designed for thermal cycling and thermal shock.

Some bakers have found baking steels to be very effective. Baking steels are more expensive but extremely durable.

20. Misting Spray

There are many ways to get steam into the oven for baking. The simplest and safest is to use a water spray bottle. When water is misted into the oven it quickly becomes steam. An inexpensive misting bottle can be used to provide an initial injection of steam into the oven when the dough is placed in the oven. The surface of the dough can also be misted to improve the crust formation.

21. Digital probe thermometer

For accuracy and repeatability in baking, a digital probe thermometer is very useful. It can be used to check dough temperatures during fermentation as well as final baking temperatures.

22. Infra-red thermometer

Checking the temperature of a baking stone is easy with an infra-red thermometer. This can also be used to check the temperature of liquids.

23. Mixing spoons

A range of spoons will be useful: from teaspoons for scooping seeds and spices, to wooden mixing spoons for mixing ingredients and initial mixing of the dough.

24. Dough Whisk

Sometimes dough will start too wet to use hands. Sometimes using a mixing spoon is too much work. At times like these, a stainless-steel dough whisk (Danish dough whisk) is very useful.

25. Stand Mixer

A solid stand mixer with a dough hook is a very useful piece of equipment when preparing some doughs, especially panettone and croissant dough.

26. Saucepans

For bathing, or dipping dough like bagels, doughnuts and pretzels, a 2-litre or 3-litre saucepan is needed. A smaller saucepan is useful for warming milk or for preparing scald.

27. Coffee mill or food processor

A mill with blades, rather than burrs, is good for milling spices, as well as chia or flax seeds.

28. Pastry brush

There are many types of pastry brush available. I prefer brushes that can be thoroughly cleaned to remove food residues.

29. Baking paper

This is useful for lining baking trays, especially where fat, fruit or some other filling is likely to leak from the dough during baking. When baking most free-form bread, dusting the peel or tray is a satisfactory method of preventing dough from baking onto the baking tray or stone.

30. Sandwich Press

A sandwich press, preferably a press with two flat plates, is needed for making the wraps featured on page 87.

31. Sealable boxes and containers

Glass containers are useful, especially for preparing and storing starters, but there is always the risk of breaking them. Plastic containers should always be food grade plastic. Plastic bowls and boxes for mixing and fermenting dough can be covered with a lid, or with a damp cloth to prevent the surface of the dough drying.

31. Skewers

When panettone is to be hung to cool, skewers can be very useful to provide handles. Stainless stress or bamboo skewers are suitable. Do not use chrome-plated, or other metal skewers that may corrode in a moist, slightly acidic environment.

32. Dutch oven, cloche, lidded baking dish

If the oven is not well sealed, or there are difficulties keeping steam around the baking loaf, a Dutch Oven, cloche or a lidded baking dish can be useful. The lid should be removed 15 to 20 minutes before the end of baking to allow the crust to gain a bit more colour.

33. Proving box

A working proving box doesn't have to be expensive, although you can buy sophisticated proving cabinets if you have both the need and the budget. A few inexpensive items can be used to improvise a proving box. An insulated box with a heat pack, cooling rack or bamboo sushi rolling mat and an inexpensive digital thermometer can be used to set up a simple, but effective proving box.

34. Slow cooker

A temperature-controlled cooker for making soups, pot roasts and stews can be used for preparing liquid malts.

35. Bread knife

A good, well balanced, comfortable bread knife is a worthwhile investment for slicing bread. This is one piece of equipment where it is worth spending a little more to buy a bread knife that will slice easily and comfortably for many years.

36. Breadboard

A wooden breadboard provides a safe surface on which to cut and slice bread. A food-grade polypropylene cutting board is also durable and will also protect both the bench surface, and the blade of the bread knife.

37. Flour mill

Some people may not see a flour mill as a high priority at first. I started milling my own seed after a few disasters with rancid flour and flour that was full of weevils. Learning the hard way was very disappointing and expensive. I dislike waste, and throwing out food. The price of mills was much higher when I bought my first mill, but I still saved money by milling flour. Since then I have been milling wonderful flour that is fresh, tastier, more nutrotious, and much cheaper than I can buy. See page 23 for information about milling.

38. Records

Make notes in a way that makes sense to you so that you can return to the notes, check what you have done and what you have observed and what you have learned. You may prefer paper or digital note-taking.

Milling flour

Why mill your own flour?

At first, the notion of milling flour is daunting. Many questions arise, and it is easier to consign the idea to the 'too hard' bin! In reality, milling your own flour is not as difficult or as expensive as it may seem, and there are many benefits that come with milling. Those benefits include:

- having a regular supply of fresh flour when you need it
- using all the nutrients available in the seed
- making flour from any gluten-free seed you can buy
- preparing flour mixes that are not available to buy
- reducing the cost of making your own gluten-free bread
- having more control over the gluten-free status of you food.

Cost

If you invest in a flour mill your investment will return many benefits, including less expensive flour. When I bought my first mill it saved me enough within a year to pay for itself, and I was only baking once or twice a week.

Fresh flour

We can always use fresh flour — notice I say fresh flour, not fresher flour. This is because when we mill, we have the opportunity of milling only the flour we are using now. As soon as flour is milled the oils from the germ of the seed begini to oxidize. If the flour is stored the oils gradually become rancid. This begins to affect the flavour of the flour as rancid oils become bitter.

When flour is milled as it is required there is no longer any need to store flour. Having to make food from a limited, poor quality, degraded flour is a thing of the past. Now we can prepare fresh, live flour and use it immediately, gaining all the nutritional benefits available from fresh flour.

A wider variety of flours

The range of seeds that can be turned into flour is extensive. Not only rice, quinoa, and buckwheat, but also millet, corn, amaranth, sorghum, and also all the varieties of those seeds. With a mill, we can have flours that are not available to buy.

If we look at rice there is not only white and brown rice, but also red, black and purple rice, short, medium, and long grain rice; rice with different proportions of natural starches. I mill arborio rice for doughs that are smooth, and creamy. Sushi rice provides a good intermediate between medium or long grain rice flour and sweet or sticky rice flour.

There is a world of millets: yellow, red, foxtail, pearl, brown top, and many more, all with different characteristics to try in your doughs.

We can also prepare flour from nuts, like chestnuts and from pulses like lentils, peas and beans. This gives an even wider range of flours, flour properties and flavours.

Reduced risks

The risk of cross-contamination with gluten grains is much easier to manage, as you can see and remove stray seeds if there is a problem with your supply being contaminated.

Storing seed

Seeds naturally and inherently have a long storage life if they are kept in cool dry conditions. It is easier to manage a collection of seeds kept at peak condition than it is to manage a collection of flours. If gluten-free seed is bought in bulk (for convenience, and to make further savings) it should be stored in containers and locations that prevent insect or rodent damage. Paper or plastic bags are not substantial enough for longer-term seed storage. Sealable food grade plastic containers are satisfactory for storing seed for a few months at a time.

Using a mill

Whatever mill you choose, whether it is a hand mill or a powered mill, be sure to follow the manufacturer's use and care instructions. If you want to improvise, for your own safety, please work within the limits set by the manufacturer's instructions. Take time to get to know your mill. Each mill has its own characteristics. So, take your time to learn how to get the best out of your mill.

Milling fine flour

Many doughs require fine, but not extra-fine flour. Other doughs require very fine flours to perform at their best.

To mill the finest flour, it may be necessary to sift and re-mill the coarse matter from your flour. With the Hawos Billy 100 (my first powered mill) I found this was the only way to get the finer flours needed for developing some of my more challenging bread formulas. The Hawos instructions recommend against re-milling flour as the flour may clog up the mill. So, milling on a medium setting, then sifting, then re-milling only the coarse material on the finest setting. This is the best method I have found that allows me to produce the finest flour with the Hawos mill.

With the MockMill 100 and 200 sifting is not necessary. The flour is milled 2 or three times on successively finer settings:

- For hard millet seeds, I mill first at #5, then #1
- For rice and larger hard seeds, like sorghum, I mill at #10, then #5, then #1

Another practice for producing the finest flour with a powered mill is reducing the flow of seed into the mill-stones. This can be done by setting the mill-stones to their finest setting, then hand feeding the seed into the hopper. This method can reduce the throughput, and allows the mill to produce, in one pass, the finest flour the mill can produce.

As an alternative to hand feeding the seed, I have made a folded cone or funnel using light cardboard. It has a 12mm diameter hole for the seed to feed into the throat of the mill. The card cone sits in the mill hopper. The mill is switched on and adjusted to the finest setting. Next, the seed is poured into the cone. Sometimes rice grains clog the hole of the cone. This happens because of the shape of rice grains. A quick tap to the cone restores the flow of rice.

Promise & Fulfilment - real bread without gluten

Choosing leaven

When we know what sort of bread we want to bake, choosing the leaven is our first step. If we are using some form of natural ferment it must be prepared. Even if it is bought, some preparation is usually required. If we choose bakers' yeast or baking soda we must still get it from somewhere.

Many ways to raise dough

There are many different approaches to making bread dough rise. Natural fermentation was used to leaven bread through most of history. Since the industrial revolution, and more particularly in the 20th century, two other leavens came into common use: bakers' yeast and baking soda.

Bakers' yeast can be seen as a refinement of natural fermentation. A particular yeast, *Saccharomyces cerevisiae*, selected from beer barm (a by-product from brewing beer) has been refined and developed to produce a fast-acting yeast. This yeast is commonly used in industrial bakeries and many domestic kitchens to produce particular types of bread, usually using highly refined ingredients. Bakers' yeast uses the same mechanisms that are used by yeasts in natural fermentation, but the population of yeast cells is orders of magnitude higher than what we might find in a naturally fermented dough. Rapid leavening of breads with bakers' yeast can be attractive as a means of getting a product ready quickly. However rapid processes don't allow adequate time for other biological and chemical processes that provide character and flavour to bread.

Baking soda was introduced to the world of food and baking in the mid 1800s a result of the industrial revolution. It became widely available as a food ingredient in the late 1800s. Baking soda and other chemical leavening agents rely on chemical reactions to produce gases that raise the dough. Chemical leavens are useful for people who cannot consume yeasts. However, the rapid rising of soda breads does not allow time for flours and other ingredients in the dough to be transformed by enzymes, bacteria, and yeasts to the more digestible forms available from long fermentation.

Steam and air can be used as leavening agents where the dough is cooked at high temperatures, as well as when the dough has been prepared using techniques that entrap air in the dough or batter. These techniques may include mechanical techniques like whisking or beating, as well as folding and laminating the dough.

Fermenting dough

Fermented cultures can be liquid or stiff. Liquid cultures can range from yeast waters to very high hydration sourdough cultures. The differences, apart from the amount of water added to the dough, are in the microbes that dominate during fermentation. Yeast waters intentionally use sugars to ensure that yeasts dominate. Some microbes do better in wetter environments, others seem to manage well when there is less water available. Cultures are generally prepared at around 100% hydration (1 part flour to 1 part water, by weight). The ferment is then refreshed at the same level, or a higher level of hydration.

With both liquid starters and stiff cultures, temperature also influences both the rate of fermentation and the microbes that dominate. Each flour has its own community of microbes that originate from the plant and the place where the seed was grown. The microbes have a preference for the food provided by the host plant. Some microbes are collected on the way from the field to the bakery, as well as in the bakery from the environment and from people. Managing the microbes in the bread, what the microbes do, and how they do it, is part of the baker's task. For most of us this is an art learned by trial, error and inference more than by scientific investigation.

Under the right conditions fermentation will occur in most materials and substances around us. When we talk about natural fermentation of food, we are talking about a carefully controlled and managed fermentation of particular food products that are fermented by enzymes, bacteria and yeasts. The enzymes we find in our flours are part of the seeds the flour is milled from. Their original role is to act in the process of germinating the seed.

The soils that grow our foods are living communities that include lactic acid bacteria and other bacteria, as well as yeasts, moulds and fungi. Some of the bacteria and yeasts present with the seeds, and the flours, may have their origins in the soils where the seeds were grown. The bacteria and yeasts in our flours are those usually associated with the plants the seeds come from, and the environments in which they are produced. The bacteria and yeasts may also be present in the seed as part of a symbiotic relationship. It is likely that they also have roles to play in the germination of seeds and the establishment of young seedlings. When we mix water with flour to preapre a starter culture we are harnessing the systems that were developed to grown plants.

Not all nutrients in seeds, or microbes associated with them, are healthy for humans to eat. Some of the nutrients are not available to us because they are chemically bound and require the germination or fermentation process to make them available. Some microbes can cause illness. Fermentation of flour in starters and in bread dough can work to make bread safe and nutritious. Fermentation breaks down and reduces the quantity of phytates and other compounds can be indigestible or potentially toxic to humans in large quantities. The process of natural fermentation, in some cases, also lowers the glycaemic index of the dough by reducing the quantity starches which are readily converted to sugars. The sugars are converted to acids and gases that assist in leavening the dough, as well as providing other benefits to the dough. Types of natural fermentation of bread dough include 'sourdough' cultures, yeast waters, barms, scobies and tibicos.

Dough can also be fermented with intentionally selected and prepared strains of microbes, like those in bakers' yeast. Bakers' yeast is usually a selected strain of the yeast *saccharomyces cerevisiae*. While the *saccharomyces cerevisiae* is common in the environment and is likely to be found in most natural fermentation mixtures, the strains prepared as bakers' yeast have been bred and carefully selected for their ability to work rapidly in particular environments. Preparations of bakers' yeast are commonly available in dried forms as dried yeast, instant yeast, and instant dried yeast. It can also be bought as a cake of fresh yeast.

Sourdough

Sourdough is produced by culturing flour and water. Culturing a sourdough starter takes week or more to ensure that a stable and robust starter is produced. It is possible to make a range of cultures, each from a distinct gluten free flour, each with its own characteristic microbes, flavours, aromas, and activity.

Although it is possible to buy sourdough cultures, or even receive a gift from another baker or a friend, developing a sourdough culture is an interesting and worthwhile exercise. There are several benefits to developing a sourdough culture. First, you know exactly what ingredients went into the culture. You may even know the provenance of the flour, what variety it is, where it was grown and how it was grown. You may even have the privilege of knowing the farmer who grew it! Second, when you develop a sourdough culture you get to know your culture: you see changes as it develops and matures. As you become familiar with its changes, you learn how it should be, and are better prepared to notice unhealthy changes if they occur. You also learn how robust the starter is, and you learn how to care for the culture.

As a sourdough culture develops it will become a complex community of bacteria and yeasts. Some of these may have a symbiotic relationship, producing compounds that enhance the environment for each other.

To prepare a sourdough culture the only ingredients required are flour and water. There is no need to use additional ingredients to increase the acidity, or to provide microbes to get a quick start culture. Extra ingredients may even be detrimental to developing a stable and mature culture. Though rapid preparation of a culture is attractive

from the point of view of saving time, there are a number trade-offs:

- additional ingredients bring with them other organisms and flavours
- there is not the opportunity to develop a deeper knowledge of the starter
- additives can make it difficult to notice if or when the starter is degrading

Note, however, that choosing water for your culture **is** important because treated water from the town supply may reduce the activity of your starter culture. In addition, water collected from a rainwater tank (run-off from the roof) or an unmanaged water supply may contain bacteria from bird droppings, or other biological, or chemical matter that will contaminate your starter culture.

Filtered water, boiled water (boiled then cooled), or bottled water are probably the best options for preparing a culture. If water from a rainwater tank, or unmanaged supply is the only water available, it should be boiled and cooled before being used to prepare, or to feed the culture.

A step by step method for preparing a sourdough culture can be found on page 33.

The characteristics of the cultures

Buckwheat can be the most challenging of cultures to start and to maintain. It takes the same time as other gluten free flours to prepare a mature culture but appears to be less active. This is because buckwheat starter is richer in lactic acid bacteria and has very little yeast.[1] Under some conditions buckwheat can also deteriorate rapidly. Some people find the aroma of the buckwheat, or the associated sourdough culture, too strong for their liking.The aroma of the buckwheat culture has strong earthy notes. It is generally more acidic than other gluten free cultures and can be used produce a strongly sour bread.

Millet and sorghum tend to be fruity and yeasty, not unlike beer. Quinoa tends to be nutty and earthy with some fruity overtones. Brown rice tends to be fruity and sweet, not unlike a light white wine, perhaps a chardonnay. Teff tends to be slightly earthy with chocolate overtones, especially brown teff.

Each culture provides its own contribution to the dough and the final bread. Although substitutions can be made the result will vary from mildly different, to quite different. While quinoa, brown rice, millet, sorghum and teff starters can be substituted without significant effect on the final bread, buckwheat is in a class of its own. Teff can be fermented spontaneously in two days to make 'injera'. This may be due to *Saccharomyces cerevisiae* and *Candida glabrata* being present in teff starter.[2]

---

1   Moroni, A.V., Elke, K.A., Fabio Dal Bello. Biodiversity of lactic acid bacteria and yeasts in spontaneously-fermented buckwheat and teff sourdoughs. *Food Microbiology*, 28 (2011) https://bit.ly/2UjFHlx (accessed 22 Apr, 2019)
2   ibid

This method provided on page 33 works well for preparing millet, quinoa, brown rice, sorghum, teff and buckwheat cultures.

If you prefer to have one starter, and only one starter, make it quinoa. Apart from having a lovely flavour profile, quinoa is also the most robust, generous and forgiving culture. Quinoa is quick to establish a mature culture and it is always ready to perform. I have left quinoa sealed in a jar in the refrigerator for months and retrieved a starter that is quick to return to work and performs well with the minimum of maintenance. It appears that these qualities in a quinoa starter come from the microbiology of the seeds themselves.[3] There are bacteria that enable the quinoa seeds, seedlings and plants to be very hardy, and grow well in challenging environments seem to also provide a very resilient and robust starter culture.

If you are keen to have more than one starter, then take up the challenge of a buckwheat starter. The microbes in buckwheat seem to produce more exopolysaccharides (EPS) than other starters. EPS produced by lactic acid bacteria have been shown to enhance and improve dough qualities and bread keeping qualities.[4]

Each culture has its own characteristic microbiome. The initial range of lactic acid and other bacteria, as well as yeasts associated with each culture seems to depend more on the seed and its source than other factors like the bakery environment and the microbiome of the baker. Characterising of each microbiome of each starter is a recent area of research. In time we will know more and there are likely to be many benefits from that understanding.

In this book each formula has been designed with the most suitable leaven for the bread being developed. It is possible to substitute starters. In many cases a similar result can be achieved with a different leaven. However, where buckwheat starter is used, that is the best starter for that formula. Buckwheat sourdough starter should only be replaced if you recognise that the bread may not be all you had hoped to achieve. Remember, texture, complexity of flavour of both crust and crumb are influenced by the starter, and the way the starter is managed.

Yeast Waters and Other Leavens

Yeast waters can be developed from fresh or dried fruits or vegetables, or even leaves and stems of plants. There are many approaches to preparing a yeast water. I will focus on two that I culture, that are used in formulas in this book:

raisin water, and 'bee barm' (honey yeast water). I'll also refer to one other that is used in the Buckwheat Croissants: water kefir, a symbiotic culture of yeast and bacteria. Water kefir is believed to have originated as an exudate of the *Opuntia* cactus (prickly pear) from Mexico.

Yeast waters, as the name suggests, provide more yeast activity than sourdough starters. Some yeast waters will also provide the benefits of other microbes, as they often contain a range of lactic acid and other bacteria. They can be used as a leaven in place of water, or they can be used to prepare a leaven or pre-ferment. The approach I use in the formulas in this book uses yeast waters to prepare leavens.

A leaven prepared with yeast water can provide milder flavours than a sourdough leaven, but it often lacks the depth of complex flavours available from a sourdough.

Raisin water

There are many ways to make raisin water. The simplest is this made with raisins and tepid water.

Take a sterile jar (scald the jar and lid with boiling water). When the jar has cooled put 30g organic raisins and 250g tepid water (35-37°C) in the jar. Loosely close the lid. Put the jar in a warm place and allow fermentation to start. Check the mixture 2 or 3 times a day. After three to four days, when the mixture bubbles and fizzes it is ready to use.

Raisin water can be used directly in dough as a substitute for part of the water, or it can be used to prepare a pre-ferment.[5]

'Bee barm' – honey yeast water

Honey is well known as a food with a long shelf life. It is also full of yeasts and bacteria. To make use of the yeasts and bacteria as leavening and fermenting agents in dough the honey must have water added to it. The best honey to use to begin a honey yeast culture, or bee barm, is raw honey that has never been heat treated. The process is very simple:

1.   Put a small amount, say 30g of raw, unheated honey in a sterile, glass jar.

2.   Dilute the honey with the same weight of water and mix thoroughly (30g honey, so add 30g water).

3.   Cover the jar, preferably with a sealable lid (this makes it easier to give it a shake, to check on the progress of fermentation).

4.   Allow fermentation to proceed, checking every day for bubbles by giving the jar a brief shake.

5.   When fermentation is evident add a small amount of honey, 10g, and water, 10g.

This mixture can be maintained as the 'mother', with small

3   Pitzschke, Andrea. (2016) Developmental Peculiarities and Seed-Borne Endophytes in Quinoa: Omnipresent, Robust Bacilli Contribute to Plant Fitness. *Frontiers in Microbiology.* 7. https://bit.ly/2uIJ1bn (accessed 22 Apr, 2019)

4   Lynch, Kieran & Coffey, Aidan & Arendt, Elke. (2017). Exopolysaccharide producing lactic acid bacteria: Their techno-functional role and potential application in gluten-free bread products. *Food Research International.* https://bit.ly/2HVRoce (accessed 22 Apr, 2019)

5   This method for raisin water is an adaptation of the approach provided by Emmanuel Hadjiandreaou in his book: How to Make Sourdough. London: Ryland Peters & Small. 2016

I prefer to use wilderness honey to begin the bee barm. In Tasmania, where I live, the wilderness honey is exceptionally good. There are many distinctive honey flavours that come from the native flora.

quantities being removed for a second stage of culturing with any ordinary honey. If you are maintaining a bee barm 'mother', refresh the mother each time some is taken for use in dough. This is done by replacing the amount of bee barm removed with the same amount of liquid, made of 1 part honey + 1 part water, by weight.

It is possible to switch to the commonly available filtered honey that has been heat treated when the fermentation is well established. This will be a matter of personal preference (and perhaps personal finances because good quality raw, unheated, wilderness honey can be very expensive!) Using the raw honey to begin the bee barm culture allows the available wild yeasts and bacteria to be harvested.

Bee barm can be used in two ways:

• directly in the dough: I use about 50g of the honey yeast water in a formula with 300g flour. No additional yeast or sourdough starter are required. The bee barm is counted as part of the total water in the formula

• to prepare a pre-ferment: for a strong pre-ferment use 150g honey yeast water with 100g flour; for a weaker pre-ferment (and therefore a slower fermentation) use 50g honey yeast water with 100g water and 100g flour

Fermentation of the bee barm may take some time to commence. Be patient. If you want to use bee barm it is best to begin the 'mother' culture some weeks ahead of baking with it.

Water kefir
Water kefir is believed to have originated as an exudate of the *Opuntia* cactus (prickly pear) from Mexico. The symbiotic community of yeasts and bacteria in water kefir is similar to that of flour-based sourdough starters. Water kefir, like other yeast waters, can be used directly in dough or it can be used to prepare a pre-ferment.

When it is used directly in the dough it is used to replace part, or all of the total water required in the dough. When water kefir is used to prepare a pre-ferment a mixture of water kefir and flour is used. The ratio of water kefir to flour can be 2:1, 3:2, or 1:1.

Bakers' yeast
Bakers' yeast is a strain of the yeast *saccharomyces cerevisiae* that has been isolated from beer barms which are a by-product of beer brewing. Bakers' yeast uses a much higher concentration of *saccharomyces cerevisiae* than the leavens that use so-called wild yeasts along with lactic acid bacteria. Rapid leavening of breads with bakers' yeast can be attractive as a means of getting a product ready quickly, however the rapid process doesn't allow adequate time for other biological and chemical processes that provide character and flavour to bread. Bakers' yeast can be bought in a number of forms: fresh, dried, and instant dried yeast.

Maintaining sourdough cultures
Most sourdough cultures are refreshed at 100% hydration: that is equal weights of fresh flour and water. The '100%' indicates that the weight of water is the same as the weight of flour.

It is just as important to use the freshest flour available for maintaining the starter, as it is to use the freshest flour available for building dough. The quantity of flour and water for each refresh will depend on how often a starter is used and how much is required to prepare leaven for dough. I usually keep about 80g to 100g of each 'mother' starter in individual sealed jars, in the refrigerator. If the starter has been refreshed within the past few days I take some of the starter to prepare my leaven, then refresh the 'mother' jar if necessary, leaving it on the bench to ferment for 4 hours, or so, before returning it to the refrigerator.

So long as the sourdough culture is used regularly and refreshed regularly it should be possible to make bread with that culture for years.

In a kitchen that is around 20 degrees Celsius, a newly refreshed starter will usually reach its peak between about 4 and 8 hours. Quinoa, brown rice, and millet generally take between 4 and 6 hours, whilst buckwheat tends to need longer and may even exceed 8 hours.

When starters are not being used or refreshed they may be kept in refrigerator between refreshing. Buckwheat is better refreshed more frequently than weekly. Brown rice, millet, sorghum, and teff are better refreshed every week. Quinoa may be left longer than one week before refreshing.

Preparing a leaven from the starter
For many formulas in this book a simple ratio of 1 part starter mixed with 2 parts water and 2 parts flour is all that is required.

So, for 50g quinoa leaven:

50g quinoa leaven = 10g quinoa starter + 20g water + 20g quinoa flour

Mix the ingredients in a suitable bowl or jar, cover and set the leaven aside to ferment for about 8 hours (assuming the room temperature is 20 degrees Celsius).

Where a leaven differs from this pattern clear instructions are provided in the formula.

Some formulas use 2 leavens. Using two leavens allows the baker to harness the qualities that each starter culture can bring to the dough.

See the brief discussion about the characteristics of cultures on pages 28 & 29.

Using sourdough cultures

The longer the starter is left before refreshing the more acid starter will become: this will tend to provide more sour flavours in the bread. The more frequently a starter is refreshed the less acid the starter will be in the resulting bread will be less sour, or not sour at all.

Storage and refresh temperatures will also affect the complexity of the flavours produced by the sourdough. Various lactic acid bacteria and wild yeasts in the culture will become more active at different temperatures. As a rule of thumb the longer the fermentation time, and the cooler the ferment the more sour the final bread.

To reduce the time for dough fermentation: add more starter, increase the hydration, and increase the temperature for fermentation.

To increase the time for dough fermentation: reduce the amount of starter, reduce the hydration and reduce the temperature of fermentation.

Preparing cultures for storage or travel

There are two challenges for the baker who travels. The first is how to prepare the sourdough culture for a rest while we travel. The second is how to travel with a sourdough culture. Everyone has their preferred approach.

Drying starter is a popular method. To do this a mature starter is spread thinly on baking paper and dried. The dried starter can be crumbled packed in an airtight container for travel or for storage. To activate the starter, it is mixed with some water to make a paste, and then refreshed as normal. I find that drying changes the balance of bacteria and yeast in the starter, and the revived starter behaves a little differently.

Refrigerating a starter at normal (100%) hydration is fine for short periods, say a week or two.

To refrigerate for longer times the starter culture can be prepared by mixing a low hydration refresh. This is a simple way of reducing the liquid, and therefore the activity of the culture. A stiff, dry paste is prepared and sealed in an

If you are travelling across international borders you may need to consider the border control arrangements and requirements of the countries you will visit. It must be better to declare and lose the precious starter than to conceal and face the consequences when discovered.

airtight container. This can be stored in the refrigerator for two to three times the usual refrigerated storage for the culture. To activate the starter, it is transferred to a larger, sterile container, and mixed with some water to the usual consistency. It should revive in the same way as a normal refresh.

For longer periods of inactivity or for travel the starter culture can be prepared by making a very dry mix of the usual flour for the starter and no water. First a stiff dry paste is prepared, and then more flour is added to prepare a dry crumble. The dry crumble is packed tightly into an airtight container. It can be frozen or prepared for travel. If it is to be frozen allow it to rest for an hour or so before freezing. To re-activate the starter transfer it to a larger, sterile container and mix in some water to the usual consistency. It should revive in the same way as a normal refresh, but if it seems a bit sluggish after 8 hours refresh it again.

Chemical leavening agents

This group includes sodium bicarbonate (bi-carb soda or bicarbonate of soda) and 'baking powders' as well as steam and air. Some yeast free leavening agents are chemical mixtures that rely on an acid and a base to generate gases, mainly carbon dioxide, during the mixing and baking phases. Baking powders often rely on sodium bicarbonate as well as other chemical compounds such as: ammonium bicarbonate, potassium bicarbonate, or potassium bitartrate (cream of tartar).

Bread prepared with chemical leavening is not considered to be 'real bread', however some people are not able to tolerate yeasts. For this reason, 2 soda bread formulas that use minimal amounts of bicarbonate of soda for leavening have been included on pages 149 to 153 of this book.

Preparing sourdough cultures

This method works well for preparing millet, quinoa, brown rice, sorghum, teff and buckwheat cultures. The dominant aroma is different with each. Millet tends to be fruity and yeasty, not unlike beer. Quinoa tends to be nutty and earthy with some fruity overtones. Brown rice tends to be fruity and slightly sweet, not unlike a light white wine, perhaps a chardonnay. Buckwheat tends to be slightly sweet and grassy with earthy notes. Teff tends to be slightly earthy with chocolate overtones, especially brown teff. Teff can be fermented spontaneously in two days to make 'Injera', however, to prepare a starter culture I prefer to follow the process of maturing the culture to ensure it is a stable culture for long term use.

Ingredients

250 grams flour (millet or quinoa or brown rice or sorghum or buckwheat or teff)
250 grams water—spring water, filtered water, or cooled boiled water

Method

Day 1   Sterilize a glass tumbler or small measuring jug and a teaspoon.
Mix 30g flour and 30g water into a smooth paste in the glass container using the sterilized teaspoon.
When mixing is finished, remove the spoon and taste the starter.
Cover the container with a lid.
Use a rubber band to indicate the level of the mixture. This will help you to see when the culture begins to be active.
Day 2   First, observe the starter. It may be possible to see some bubbles beginning to form in the starter.
Remove the cover and smell the starter, unless the ambient temperature is over 26 degrees Celsius, it is unlikely that there will be any change in the aroma. If the temperature is warm, you may detect a slightly 'fruity' aroma.
Sterilize a teaspoon and add 30g of water to the starter and mix well. Add 30g of flour and mix well into the starter.
When mixing is finished, remove the spoon and taste the starter.
Move the 'marker' rubber band to the new level of the starter.
Day 3   Observe the starter. It may be possible to see some bubbles beginning to form in the starter.
Remove the cover and smell the starter, you may notice a faint fruity aroma.
Sterilize a teaspoon and add 30g of water to the starter and

mix well. Add 30g of flour and mix well into the starter.
When mixing is finished, remove the spoon and taste the starter.
Move the 'marker' rubber band to the new level of the starter.
Day 4   Observe the starter. There should now be bubbles forming in the starter. The bubbles may be very small.
Remove the cover and smell the starter, you may notice a fruity aroma.
The starter culture should have increased in size and the top surface should have risen well above the 'marker'.
Refresh the starter by removing all except about 2 tablespoons of the culture with a sterilized teaspoon.
Add 30g of water to the starter and, with a clean, sterilized spoon mix well. Add 30g of flour and mix well into the starter.
When mixing is finished, remove the spoon and taste the starter.
Move the 'marker' rubber band to the new level of the starter.
Days 5, 6, & 7   The starter culture should have increased in size and the top surface should have risen above the 'marker'. Repeat the activity from Day 4.
Day 8
The starter should now be ready to use.
When you remove some starter to make your sourdough bread use a sterilized spoon.

Refresh the starter by adding equal weights of water and flour.

Preparing lievito madre

Lievito Madre is a natural yeast product prepared in an Italian tradition. It is a stiff sourdough starter. Lievito is yeast, madre is mother. Some bakers use the name interchangeably with pasta (dough) madre. The 'mother' indicates the original yeast source that provides life again and again and again to bread. The mother, fed, refreshed, and cared for with great diligence continues to provide the life to a range of breads.

Typically, lievito madre is prepared as a stiff dough and fermented in a tight linen roll, or in a water bath. Fermenting in the tight roll produces a more acid dough, whereas the bath reduces the acidity by leaching the acidic compounds from the dough.

The result of a bathed or washed lievito madre is an active, thoroughly fermented dough with a very mild flavour. The washed lievito madre is used for panettone or other enriched doughs like brioche and croissants, as well as pizza.

Preparing a lievito madre is counter-intuitive to the gluten-free baker. In the world of gluten-baking, washing lievito madre is possible because of the gluten that holds the dough together. However, as we learn about the qualities of gluten-free flours and sours, we can see that it is possible to prepare a lievito madre without gluten. The exercise of preparing dry starters for storage or travelling provides a few clues to the process (see page 31). However, none

of the sours on its own would make a malleable dough. When at least two of the sours are combined things change. By adding a third we have a malleable dough that can be fermented in a tight roll.

Fermenting a stiff starter in a roll is one thing, washing that starter is quite a different challenge. The dough will dissolve in a water bath. Gums or a high fibre ingredient like psyllium could be added to stabilize the dough. Unfortunately these additives are water soluble, which means that the dough would still dissolve into the water bath. Using additives would also create a complex problem for calculating the percentages of flours and additive during refreshing. A different approach is needed.

We need an approach that preserves the integrity of the dough, and also permits leaching of the acids in a simple and manageable way. To prevent the dough from falling apart during washing I use a single layer of butter muslin.

When the dough is prepared it is first flattened (hands or a rolling pin can be used), then rolled up into a stout log. The log is stood in the middle of a square of clean butter muslin and the cloth is gathered around the dough. The cloth is twisted and wrapped around at the top. The lievito madre is left to mature in the water bath for at least three hours. During this time the dough can be removed, and the water changed. Changing the water will allow the acidity of the dough to be further reduced.

Preparation

To prepare lievito madre without gluten, we need starters that produce plenty of exopolysaccharides (EPS), the gel that forms in starters. Each starter seems to produce its own type of EPS, so a mix of starters has the potential to provide the qualities that are needed for forming a stable dough. I divide my starters into two groups: the primary starters which produce more EPS; and the secondary starters that produce less but have other properties. Buckwheat and quinoa are primary because of their qualities for forming a dough. Brown rice, millet, sorghum and teff are secondary starters. Each of the secondary starters has useful qualities. Currently, my preference for the secondary starter is millet which makes a firmer dough.

The initial mix of sours for lievito madre is 50g each of the following sourdough starters: buckwheat, quinoa, and millet. A mixture of the same flours consisting of 50g each of buckwheat, quinoa, and millet is added. The flours should be whole grain, and as fine as possible. Mix the flours and sours well.

At first the dough will be dry and slightly crumbly. Knead the dough for a few minutes. During the kneading the dough will soften and become more malleable.

When the dough is quite soft and pliable shape the dough as a slab about 5mm thick. Next roll the slab into a stout log. Wrap the dough by placing the base of the log in the centre of a 30cm x 30cm square of butter muslin. Gather the muslin around the dough log and twist the loose ends around. The corners of the cloth are gathered together and twisted, then wrapped around the top of the log to form a 'bun'.

A length of cotton string can be used to tie the cloth, keeping the dough log in the muslin cloth, however if the winding is done well string should not be needed.

To prepare the lievito madre for dry fermenting, it should then be wrapped firmly in a stout piece of calico or linen and tied in a firm parcel.

When the lievito madre is to be washed or wet fermented it should be placed in a bowl of fresh water. The muslin wrapped dough should be gently placed in to the water; it should not have water poured over it as this will cause flour to leach from the cloth cover. Initially the dough will sink to the bottom of the bowl, but as the dough ferments it will become buoyant and eventually float at the top. The bath water can be changed periodically to reduce the acidity of the dough. It can be bathed for up to 24 hours on the bench (this depends on the room temperature), or longer in the refrigerator. When the dough is floating freely at the top of the water the dough is ready for use, or for refreshing.

Using test papers, I have sampled the bath water to find the pH of the water decreases from pH 7 to around pH 4 if the bath water is not changed. Even when it is changed, the pH of the water will readily reduce to pH 5.5. This indicates that the acids are leaching from the fermenting dough.

Refreshing lievito madre

To refresh the lievito madre we must consider two different approaches, depending on how it has been fermented:

Dry fermented: the dough is bound in a cloth and tied firmly to ferment.

When lievito madre is dry fermented, take the initial 100g of lievito madre and add 75g water and a further 50g of each flour: buckwheat, quinoa, and millet. This will provide a refreshed starter of 325g at about 45% hydration.

Wet fermented: the dough is wrapped in butter muslin and floated in a water bath.

When lievito madre is fermented wet, place the initial, mature 100g of dough in a medium mixing bowl and add 50g of each flour: buckwheat, quinoa, and millet. Begin by working the flour into the dough. There are two possible outcomes. Either the dough will be too soft to work into a

roll, or the dough will be too dry and crumbly to work.

First, if the dough comes together as a very soft dough, then add small amounts of buckwheat flour and quinoa flour until the dough becomes firmer and can be worked into a malleable dough.

Second, if the dough is dry and crumbly after the flour has been worked in, add very small amounts of water until the dough becomes softer and can be worked into a malleable dough.

Using lievito madre

Formulas for challah, cinnamon scrolls, panettone, wholegrain croissants and brioche feuilettée in this book require 200g of washed lievito madre. To use it at its peak requires the madre to be refreshed three times. This will generate excess from the first and second refreshes, unless the lievito madre is being multiplied for a large bake. The excess generated by washing is suitable for use in pizza dough (page 85) or crumpets (page 197). The excess can also be used in most other bread formulas if the hydration is adjusted to suit the formula.

For pizza dough lievito madre may be washed or dry fermented.

Storing lievito madre

The dough can be wrapped in butter muslin and stored in a jar at room temperature for a few days, or in the refrigerator for longer periods. The storage jar should have plenty of space around the dough as the dough will expand.

For longer term storage lumps of about 100g of the dough can be rolled into a ball and stored, without wrapping, in an airtight jar in a refrigerator. I prefer a glass jar because it makes monitoring the balls of starter easier, and there is no need to open the jar.

Storage is a simple matter of preparing a refresh, rolling the dough into a tight ball, or a number of tight balls and storing the balls in a sealed, clear jar in the refrigerator. I find that making 100g balls is a good approach as it is easy to see how much lievito madre dough is in storage. Some fermentation will continue during storage, so be aware that there will be a build-up of pressure in the storage jar.

After storage use the **Dry fermented** refreshing method to prepare the lievito madre for either dry or wet fermentation.

Sourdough starter diary

Starter name	

Flour ○ Quinoa ○ Brown Rice ○ Millet ○ Sorghum ○ Teff ○ Buckwheat

Day 1 Date / / Time : Temp °C/°F	**Day 5** Date / / Time : Temp °C/°F
Ingredients added grams water grams flour	**Ingredients added** grams water grams flour
Observations	**Observations**
Colour	Colour
Texture	Texture
Aroma	Aroma
Taste	Taste
Notes	**Notes**
Day 2 Date / / Time : Temp °C/°F	**Day 6** Date / / Time : Temp °C/°F
Ingredients added grams water grams flour	**Ingredients added** grams water grams flour
Observations	**Observations**
Colour	Colour
Texture	Texture
Aroma	Aroma
Taste	Taste
Notes	**Notes**
Day 3 Date / / Time : Temp °C/°F	**Day 7** Date / / Time : Temp °C/°F
Ingredients added grams water grams flour	**Ingredients added** grams water grams flour
Observations	**Observations**
Colour	Colour
Texture	Texture
Aroma	Aroma
Taste	Taste
Notes	**Notes**
Day 4 Date / / Time : Temp °C/°F	**Day 8** Date / / Time : Temp °C/°F
Ingredients added grams water grams flour	**Ingredients added** grams water grams flour
Observations	**Observations**
Colour	Colour
Texture	Texture
Aroma	Aroma
Taste	Taste
Notes	**Notes**

Baking record

Bread Description				Record #	
Start Date	**Start Time**		**End Date**	**End Time**	
Room Temperature			**Room Temperature**		
Milling	flour	grams	flour	grams	flour	grams
	flour	grams	flour	grams	flour	grams
Leaven	starter	grams	water	grams	flour	grams
2nd Leaven	starter	grams	water	grams	flour	grams

Notes on leaven(s):

Dough	leaven	grams	**Schedule**	**Temperatures**
Notes on dough:	2nd leaven	grams	am/pm leaven ready	
	flour	grams	am/pm dough rest	dough temp
	flour	grams	am/pm fermenting	dough temp
	flour	grams	am/pm shaping	dough temp
	flour	grams	am/pm proving	dough temp
	flour	grams	am/pm preheat oven	oven temp
	flour	grams	am/pm baking	oven temp
	water	grams	am/pm end baking	oven temp
	salt	grams		internal temp
	hydrocolliod	grams	am/pm cooling start	
	hydrocolliod	grams		
		grams	**Observations:**	
		grams		
		grams		
		grams		
		grams		
		grams		
	Total dough weight:	grams	**Baked weight:**	grams

Comments:

Shaping and scoring

Shaping

Shaping free-form dough appears straightforward but requires some thought and care. In free form loaves, baguettes and even rolls the crust is an integral part of the structure of the bread. The dough is shaped and formed to create a slight tension in the crust. No, there is no gluten, but the starches and polysaccharides work together to form the crust and that can hold a low level of tension.

For some doughs, like baguettes, enriched doughs and pizza dough, a little pre-shaping allows the dough to be worked easily into the desired shape of the bread. A baguette can be pre-shaped as a finger-bun, rested for 15 to 30 minutes, then rolled and worked into its final baton shape. Pizza dough is pre-shaped as a ball, rested for 15 minutes, shaped as a small, thick disc, rested again, then finally shaped to the full disc. With pizza dough, the disc should have a slightly thicker perimeter to allow for a risen perimeter crust that makes it easier to handle the pizza when it is baked.

For other doughs, there is no need to pre-shape, and the fermented dough can be gently flattened, then rolled to a log shape or a ball, dusted lightly and placed in a proving basket or in the folds of a *couche*. If the shaped dough is placed in a proving basket or a *couche* it is usually placed with the joining seem uppermost. If it is placed in a bread pan the joining seam is usually placed down on the base of the bread pan.

When the dough is proved in a proving basket or *couche*, the outer skin that has been in contact with the cloth or wood fibres dries a little. This drying of the outer skin provides strength to hold the expanding dough during its final fermentation or 'proving'. If the dough is proved and baked

in a bread pan or paper bread form the surfaces in contact with the container do not dry to the same extent and remain more flexible and pliable during the first stage of the bake.

As the dough bakes the outer skin initially becomes slightly elastic as the steam and heat work on the starches in the skin to gelatinize them. As the gelatinized starches set the skin becomes the crust, providing a structure that contains the crumb as it expands during baking. As the dough is heated in the oven the moisture becomes steam and along with gases in the dough, they expand causing the dough to rise one last time. This final rise is known as 'oven spring'. It usually happens during the first 15 minutes of baking.

During baking the starches and polysaccharides inside the dough also change and gelatinize, forming the crumb. If the dough is not baked long enough the gelatinized starches do not set in the shape they have been formed into by the pressure of steam and gas. The part of the crumb that has not set will collapse.

As the crust forms, it will stretch as far as it can to accommodate the expanding crumb. Eventually, weaknesses in the crust tear open when the strength of the expanding crumb exceeds the strength of the crust.

To prevent the crust from tearing, the dough is prepared to allow controlled expansion of the crumb. This preparation begins with decisions about how the dough should be allowed to expand. Three main approaches are taken:

- the skin is cut or scored to allow expansion

- the dough is folded and shaped with seams or joins up so that they form natural sites for the dough to expand

- the dough is proved longer so the risk of tearing is minimized.

Scoring

When the aim is to develop a strong crust and an open crumb, we score the upper skin of the dough to encourage controlled expansion (oven spring) during baking.

During the final rise or oven spring, the scoring pattern controls the expansion of the dough and can avoid unplanned tears in the crust. Scoring may be a single cut, or many cuts arranged to provide decorative patterns. The location, depth and direction of cuts influence the shape, and size of the final loaf. Wise scoring on the top dough skin may help a wet dough to stand tall. Poorly considered scoring on the sides of the dough skin may result in a strong dough spreading out like a pancake!

The upper skin of the dough is scored to provide intentional weak spots where the crumb can expand. The score should suit the design of the loaf. To achieve an ear, the scoring is usually done at an angle of 30 to 35 degrees from horizontal. This angle undercuts the skin and encourages the formation of 'ears' as the dough expands and opens up the cut. The depth of the score should be in proportion to the loaf, so a baguette should be shallow, about 5mm deep. With a large rustic loaf, the score might be 15mm or even 20mm deep.

Scoring the loaf can also involve creating patterns that control expansion of the crumb as the loaf bakes. To score an intricate design across the surface of the loaf the balde should be perpendicular to the surface, and quite shallow, only 1mm to 2mm deep. This allows each score to open as the crumb expands. If scoring is an even depth the pattern will be even. If some scores are deep and others shallow the deeper scores will open more than the shallower scores.

Whether it is done for presentation, or simply to prevent a random tear, scoring is always deliberate and designed to control the way the loaf expands during baking. The direction, shape, length, depth and placement of each score influences the final shape of the loaf as much as the composition and hydration of the loaf.

No scoring

If the dough is shaped by folding, as is the case with ciabatta and other rustic loaves, the seam remains on the top or the side of the loaf allow the dough to expand at the seam.

Some enriched doughs are allowed to prove longer so that the strength of oven spring is less, and the crust is not torn. Others are shaped by braiding.

Seeded crusts

Seeded crusts also allow scope for creative design. About 50g of sesame seed, poppy seed, millet, or quinoa seeds can be used to form a crisp crust with added flavour. Roll the dough in the seeds before placing it in the proving basket. There is no need to dust the basket as the seeds will absorb moisture from the dough skin and prevent the dough from sticking to the proving basket. When scoring a seeded crust, a simple length-wise slash on a batard, or a cross on a *boule* is enough scoring for a stunning seeded loaf.

Malting seeds

Malting is a process whereby the natural germination of the seed is used to initiate enzyme activity and naturally produce sugars that can be used to improve dough. By malting seed, we can produce several products. The first product of malting is 'diastatic malt'. This is milled as flour and added in small quantities to increase the enzyme activity of a dough. If the malted seed is roasted the enzyme activity is reduced or eliminated, but the malt becomes more useful as a flavouring. Liquid malt can also be produced by stewing a mixture of flour, malted flour and water.

The malting process depends on three main activities: germinating the seed, drying the germinated seed, and removing the rootlets. To produce diastatic malt flour, the dried malted seed is milled.

For malt flavourings, the seed is roasted, cooled, then milled.

For liquid malt, some flour is mixed with diastatic malt flour, roasted malt powder and water, then heated to around 70 degrees Celsius to promote enzyme activity that converts starches to sugars. The liquid malt can be filtered and further heated to remove excess moisture and form a syrup.

Germinating seed
To germinate seed, first, soak seed in water for about 8 hours. After soaking drain the seed well and place it in a dark place to germinate.

Buckwheat germinates quickly at 26 degrees Celsius. Within 2 days the root radicle should be showing. Allow the root radicle to grow to about the same length as the seed.

Seed	Temperature – degrees Celsius	Time – days for root radicles to emerge
buckwheat	26	2
millet	26	2
quinoa	30	1
sorghum	22	2

Kilning
Kilning stops germination by drying the germinated seed at about 40 degrees Celsius . A food dehydrator can be used for this, or the seed can be dried in a cool oven.

Milling

To make diastatic malt flour from the dried seeds, the rootlets are cleaned from the dried seed. This can be done by shaking the seed in a mesh bag or colander. The dried rootlets should be brittle and easily break from the seed. When the seed has had the rootlets removed, it is ready for milling. If diastatic malt flour is required it is now milled from the prepared seed. If malt powders for flavourings and colourings are required, the seeds are roasted before milling. The longer the roasting of the malted seeds the less enzyme activity will be available.

Types of dry malt

For dry malt to use as flavourings and colourings the seed is roasted in an oven at 170 degrees Celsius for before milling. The following table Provides suggested times for each colour of malt.

Roasting time	Malt colour	Uses
15 minutes	Light malt	Some flavouring, some value as diastatic
25 minutes	Medium malt	Mainly flavouring, minimal val-ue as diastatic
40 minutes	Darker malt	Flavouring only

Preparing liquid malt

To prepare liquid malt mix 30g flour, 5g diastatic malt flour, 10g darker malt powder and 360g water in a jar. Cover the jar and place it in a water bath at 70 to 75 degrees Celsius. A slow cooker set to the 'keep warm' setting is suitable. Cover the jar, place a lid over the water bath and maintain the temperature evenly as possible. Stir the liquid every half hour for two hours, then every hour. Within 8 to 10 hours the liquid should darken and have a slightly sweet flavour and aroma. The liquid malt can be cooled, and used unrefined in dough. It can also be filtered, and excess water evaporated to produce sweeter, thicker liquid malt that can be used as a sweetener in bread dough.

Liquid malt	
30g	flour
5g	diastatic malt flour
10g	darker malt flour
360g	hot water, 70°C

Quick scald-malting

By mixing flour and water the enzymes in the flour are activated. When the water is hot, around 70 degrees Celsius, and the flour/water mixture is maintained at that temperature for at least 8 hours, the scalded flour and water mixture can be malted. This malt will improve the texture of the dough by increasing the sugars available as well as by introducing some gelatinized starch into the dough at an early stage, before baking.

A few deeper thoughts ...

Hydration

Hydration is about more than simply getting the flour wet. For a seed to germinate it must first absorb moisture to break the seed dormancy. The seed absorbs moisture, activating enzymes that begin to turn starches into food for the plant embryo. When we make flour the germination process cannot take place, but the mechanisms provided for germination are still activated when moisture is mixed with the flour.

Hydration is about ensuring that moisture is absorbed by the flour. Starch is the main part of flour. Different seeds have higher or lower levels of starch. The size and shape of starch granules vary between different seeds. The starch granules must be encouraged to absorb moisture. If moisture is not adequately absorbed into the starches, we have a wet dough that is little more than starch granules and other flour particles suspended in a water mixture. While this may work for batter, it will make it difficult to form dough and may result in a wet and unsatisfactory baked loaf.

There are several ways to cause the starch to absorb moisture. The main method used to cause the starch to rapidly absorb moisture is to damage the starch granules. Starch is damaged during the milling process. When the granules are fractured, they will absorb available moisture. During kneading the action of kneading causes further damage to starch, and so increases the absorption of moisture by the starch granules.

Soaking flour at room temperature takes advantage of some of these mechanisms and causes the starch granules to slowly absorb moisture. In bread making, this method is called *autolysis* or *autolyse*. The mechanisms at work in *autolysis* are a combination of damaged starch absorbing moisture and the transformation of starches by enzymes into simpler starches and sugars.

Progressively adding moisture to the dough is another way of working the moisture into the starch. A technique called *bassinage* can be used to increase hydration of the flour in this way. Partially wetting the flour, then re-wetting the flour causes the flour to absorb more moisture. *Bassinage* mimics the progressive wetting of seed during germination. Together with kneading and progressive wetting, *bassinage* is a very effective method for hydrating the starches and producing a better dough.

When *bassinage* is used 10% of the water from the main dough is withheld from the dough during mixing. The dough is rested for about 30 minutes, then the withheld water is worked into the dough.

Both *autolysis* and *bassinage* allow the total water in the dough to be increased.

Scalding flour is a technique that mixes flour with very hot or boiling water. It speeds up hydration of the dough by causing starch granules to rapidly expand and rupture. Moisture is absorbed into the starch granules which also begin gelatinize because of the heat.

Similar to scalding is the preparation of a *tangzhong* roux. This uses less flour (typically 5 parts water to 1 part flour) to prepare a water roux that is allowed to cool before being added to the dough.

Bakers' Percentage

The bakers' percentage is a method for expressing the ratios of ingredients in a bread formula relative to the total amount of flour. In this book, I haven't used bakers' percentage extensively because the formulas are based on a minimum size of bake. It is easy to scale these formulas from that base. The method provides a simple means of scaling a formula from a small loaf to a large loaf, or vice-a-versa. It also provides a simple means of scaling from one loaf to many for larger scale production.

The way the bakers' percentage works is this:

First, everything is measured by weight or mass, not volume.

Second, the total amount of flour is set at 100%.

The quantity of every other ingredient is expressed as a percentage of the total weight of flour. The amount of water is stated as a percentage of the total flour. So, if the formula states that there is only a single flour that flour will be 100% of the flour. Several of my formulas use only buckwheat flour. Those formulas are 100% buckwheat flour. If the formula uses 300g buckwheat flour the and the hydration is set at 100%, we can see that 300g water is required.

Where bread is made with flour containing gluten, the percentage of water may range from 65% to as high as 90%. In gluten-free bread making the amount of water is typically much higher, from say 85% to 110%. It may be even higher where some seeds such as chia or flax are included as a meal or as part of a 'soaker', or where the dough has a high percentage of hydrocolloids like gums or psyllium husk.

The following tables provide a master formula for a buckwheat loaf. The natural leaven (sourdough starter) is included as one ingredient. The leaven is at 100% hydration, that is, it is made with equal weights of flour and water. In Table 1 the weights are worked out for a single loaf of about 690g of baked bread. Table 2 scales the formula to make a larger loaf. Table 3 scales the formula to make 15 of the same loaves.

The ingredients list is specified in percentages, then in commonly used weight measurements showing how the weight is calculated from the percentage.[1]

---

1   Although US or Imperial measurements are not used in this book, the examples show those units to demonstrate how versatile the bakers' percentage method is for expressing the relative amounts of ingredients in a formula.

Table 1   Master formula for a single buckwheat loaf.

Ingredient	Bakers' %	Grams (g)	g	Ounces (oz)	oz
buckwheat flour	100%	300g	300g	11oz	11.00oz
psyllium husk	4%	300g x 4/100 = 12g	12g	11oz x 4/100 = 0.44oz	0.44oz
salt	1%	300g x 1/100 = 3g	3g	11oz x 1/100 = 0.11oz	0.11oz
water	100%	300g x 100/100 = 300g	300g	11oz x 100/100 = 11oz	11.00oz
buckwheat leaven at 100% hydration	33.33%	300g x 33.33/100 = 100g	100g	11oz x 33.33/100 = 3.6oz	3.66oz
		Total dough weight	715g	**Total dough weight**	22.55oz

Table 2   Master formula adjusted for a larger single buckwheat loaf.

Ingredient	Bakers' %	Grams (g)	g	Ounces (oz)	oz
buckwheat flour	100%	500g	500g	18oz	18.00oz
psyllium husk	4%	500g x 4/100 = 20g	20g	18oz x 4/100 = 0.44oz	0.72oz
salt	1%	500g x 1/100 = 5g	5g	18oz x 1/100 = 0.11oz	0.18oz
water	100%	500g x 100/100 = 500g	500g	18oz x 100/100 = 18oz	18.00oz
buckwheat leaven at 100% hydration	33.33%	500g x 33.33/100 = 167g	167g	18oz x 33.33/100 = 3.6oz	6.00oz
		Total dough weight	1192g	**Total dough weight**	43.00oz

Table 3   Master formula scaled up to make 15 buckwheat loaves.

Ingredient	Bakers' %	Grams (g)	g	Ounces (oz)	oz
buckwheat flour	100%	4500g	4500g	160oz	160.00oz
psyllium husk	4%	4500g x 4/100 = 180g	180g	160oz x 4/100 = 6.40oz	6.40oz
salt	1%	4500g x 1/100 = 45g	45g	160oz x 1/100 = 1.60oz	1.60oz
water	100%	4500g x 100/100 = 4500g	4500g	160oz x 100/100 = 160oz	160.00oz
buckwheat leaven at 100% hydration	33.33%	4500g x 33.33/100 = 1500g	1500g	160oz x 33.33/100 = 53.33oz	53.33oz
		Total dough weight	10725g	**Total dough weight**	381.33oz

Dough volume

There are a few times when we talk about dough, or starter, doubling in size. What we are looking for is a doubling in the volume of the dough. We must remember that double volume is not the same as 'double length x double width x double height'. If the length, width and height all doubled we would have 8 times the volume! There are very few types of dough that could be expected to grow by eight times the volume. Perhaps an incredibly light, open croissant might do that!

When we expect a dough to double in volume, if the dough is free-form, we are looking for an increase of only a small amount in each of the 3 dimensions.

Think about a balloon (if only our round loaves were as even as a balloon!)

If diameter of the balloon is 10 cm, the volume of the balloon is calculated to be[1]:

$(4 \times 5 \times 5 \times 5 \times \pi) \div 3 = (500 \times 3.14) \div 3 = 524$ cm³.

If we double the size of the balloon in all directions so that the diameter is 20 cm, the volume is:

$(4 \times 10 \times 10 \times 10 \times \pi)/3 = 4{,}189$ cm³.

That's not double the volume, it is eight times the volume! So, if we expect to see a very big increase in the volume of the dough our expectation is inflated!

If the volume of the 10 cm balloon is 524 cm³, then double the volume is 1,048 cm³.

Now, if double the volume is 1,048 cm³, when we calculate the the diameter we find that it has only increased from 10 cm to 12.6 cm

So, what about when we use a loaf pan or a bread form of some type? In a loaf pan or a bread form the dough expands mainly in one direction (assuming that the dough covers the base of the pan or form). In this case, we can reasonably expect to see the dough rise to double the height if the volume has doubled.

Some words of caution regarding dough volume:

First, doubling the volume during the proving stage is easier to assess for bread baked in a pan or bread form. For free form loaves, even those proved in a proving basket, it is not easy to estimate the doubling, so we are more inclined to look for more than double the volume. If our expectation is inflated, we may allow the loaf to 'over-prove'. This may result in dough that is very delicate, and easily damaged. To avoid over-proving I find that the 'caress test' works well. Why caress? If we were working with gluten in our dough, we could use the 'poke' test and watch for a response. If we poke dough made without gluten the indentation from the poke will remain, even when the dough is well under-proved! I find that a gentle caress of the dough conveys more information than a poke. If I caress the dough I can feel if the dough is firm, or if it is beginning to yield. When the dough has increased in volume and yields slightly to a gentle caress it is ready to bake.

Second, the inherent weakness of gluten-free dough limits the extent to which the dough can expand. To hold fermentation gases, air trapped during mixing and kneading, and steam generated during baking, there must be a dough matrix capable of containing those gases. In bread without gluten the development of a dough matrix depends on:

- the hydration of fine starch granules,
- the film-forming ability of hydrocolloids and proteins, and
- the interaction of starches with fats.

Without at least two of these properties, the dough matrix will be unable to contain gases and there will be no increase in dough volume — there will be no 'rise'. For the final baked crumb to look and feel like bread, the dough matrix requires all three properties.

original dough volume

double the original dough volume

---

1   The volume of a sphere is calculated using the formula:
         volume = $(4 \times r^3 \times \pi) \div 3$
where r is the radius of the sphere (i.e. half the diameter of the sphere) and the constant $\pi = 3.14$

Gelatinization

When the dough has been well mixed and is thoroughly hydrated, and when the microbes have done their work, it is time to bake the dough. The journey to this point has been fascinating and marvellous as we have taken simple ingredients that began as seeds, mixed them with water, and worked them into a dough that has fermented. Now we commit the fermented dough to the oven where some more amazing changes take place under the influence of extreme heat. The most significant change that happens in the oven is gelatinization of the starches.

Gelatinization happens at the molecular level as hydrated starches and hydrocolloids respond to the increased heat of the environment to become glass-like. This usually happens between 60 degrees Celsius and 70 degrees Celsius, however with some hydrocolloids the gelatinization temperature my be higher. The temperature of gelatinization depends on all the ingredients in the dough. Gelatinization is not immediate. It takes time for the process to complete and for the gelatinized dough to set into its new molecular configuration.

As heat flows through the dough, the crust is the first part of the dough to undergo gelatinization. While the crust transforms the rest of the dough continues to heat. First, the microbes complete their fermentation and succumb to the increasing heat. Enzymes continue to work breaking down starches and the heat that gelatinizes the dough begins to dry the gelatinized dough, forming the crumb of the bread.

As heat flow continues through the dough, all the starches and hydrocolloids are gelatinized. It is necessary to continue heating the dough until the gelatinized material dries and sets. Inadequate time for setting results in the collapse of the unset portion of the gelatinized dough as the dough cools.

Depending on the degree of setting that has occurred this may result in the following defects in the loaf:

• the upper part of the crumb stretches and tears away from the crust

• the unset portion of the crumb collapses, forming a dense layer of dough towards the bottom of the loaf

• in the worst case, where the dough has been over fermented (over proved), the entire crumb collapses leaving a thick, slightly malty, gooey layer of collapsed crumb in the floor of the cavern.

Gelatinization is not a permanent change in the dough. After baking another change begins to take place in the bread. That change is called retrogradation. Retrogradation is part of the staling process where the starches begin to re-organize to a more crystalline structure. There are a number of methods of retrogradation and it not yet well understood. Starch retrogradation is affected by water content, storage

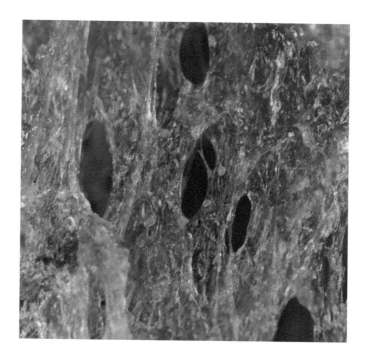

time and storage temperature, as well as additives.[1] The use of psyllium husk in the dough, as well as some fermentation products seem to have a positive effect in reducing and slowing retrogradation and staling of gluten-free bread.

---

1   Shujun Wang, Caili Li, Les Copeland, Qing Niu, Shuo Wang. Starch Retrogradation: A Comprehensive Review. *Comprehensive Review in Food Science and Food Safety*. September 2015
See https://bit.ly/2KvO4Xr (accessed 22Feb 2019)

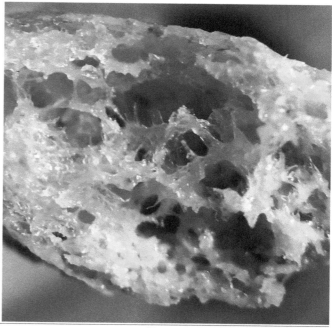

Basic bread formulas

Millet & buckwheat cottage loaf

There is little as satisfying as a good rustic loaf. The Millet & Buckwheat loaf is a wholesome bread, full of flavour and the romance of a traditional country bread.

This can be made as with a sourdough starter, or with a yeast-based preferment.

Summary

Makes: 1 loaf x 1050g

Milling: buckwheat, millet, chia, flax

Time to prepare: 20 hours

Baking time: 50 minutes

Leaven options: millet leaven or yeast

Leaven

Mix 20g millet starter with 40g water and 45g millet flour.
Cover the bowl or jug and allow the mixture to ferment for around eight hours.

Dough

In a large mixing bowl combine all the dry ingredients: 180g millet flour, 180g buckwheat flour, 50g chia meal, 30g flax meal, 10g psyllium husk, and 3g salt.
Gently with a whisk to ensure there are no lumps of chia and flax meal.

Mix 450g tepid water and 30g honey with the leaven.
Pour the leaven mixture onto the dry ingredients and combine well.

Fermenting

Cover the dough and set the dough to rise for 8 hours in a warm place.

Shaping

Dust the kneading board lightly and gently knead the dough by spreading and folding it.
Divide the dough into two lumps, one roughly 750g and 250g.
Shape dough into two balls.
Place the larger ball on a baking sheet, then place the smaller ball on the top centre of the larger ball.
Using a thumb press down through the middle of both balls to form the 'cottage'.

Proving

Cover shaped dough.
Set dough to rise for 2 hours in a warm, draft free place.
Preheat the oven to 220°C.
The loaf can be scored just before baking, if desired.

Baking

Bake in a hot oven (210°C) for 50 minutes.

Cooling

Remove the loaf from the oven and place on a rack to cool.

Variation

This variation allows the Millet & Buckwheat Cottage Loaf to be leavened with either instant yeast or fresh yeast.

Leaven

1g	instant yeast
(2g)	(fresh yeast)
45g	water
60g	fine millet flour

Activity	Time	Total
Preparing leaven	0:05	0:05
Fermenting leaven	8:00	8:05
Building dough	0:10	8:15
Fermenting	8:00	16:15
Shaping	0:05	16:20
Proving	2:00	18:20
Baking	0:50	19:10
Cooling	1:00	20:10

Leaven

20g	millet starter
40g	water
45g	fine millet flour

Dough

105g	leaven
180g	millet flour
180g	buckwheat flour
50g	chia seeds (meal)
30g	flax seeds (meal)
10g	psyllium husks
3g	salt
30g	honey
450g	tepid water

Additional buckwheat flour for dusting the workbench and the proving basket.

Quinoa sourdough

Quinoa is a seed that originated in South America. It grows well on many soil types, producing a crop of seeds that can be used in many ways. This quinoa sourdough can be made with white, red, or black quinoa, or a mixture. Usually only white quinoa is available as a flour, however if you mill your own flour your options are increased. See page 17 for information on preparing quinoa seed.

Summary

Makes: 1 loaf x 750g

Milling: quinoa

Time to prepare: 18 ½ hours

Baking time: 1 hour

Leaven: quinoa leaven

Leaven

In a medium mixing bowl mix 15g quinoa starter and 400g water.
Add 200g quinoa flour to the water and mix thoroughly. The leaven should now look like a thin batter.
Cover the bowl and set aside in a warm place to ferment. After about 4 hours there should be signs of activity.
The leaven will reach the peak of rising and then it will begin to fall somewhere between 8 and 12 hours after it was started: now is the time to make the dough.

If the leaven has separated into layers, stir to mix the layers.

Dough

In a large mixing bowl mix 150g tapioca flour, 50g quinoa flour, 12g psyllium husk, and 4g salt together. It is important to mix them thoroughly so that the psyllium husk is distributed evenly through the flour mix. Stir the flour mix into the leaven pre-ferment. Combine thoroughly.
Leave the dough to rest for at least 10 minutes.
This allows the flour and psyllium husk to absorb the water. Initially the dough will be sticky.

Shaping

Dust the work bench with a little of the 1:1 quinoa/ tapioca flour. Dust your hands with the flour mix and gently lift and spread the dough.
Gently spread and fold the dough twice. Shape the dough into a batard.

Proving

Set the batard in a proving basket to prove. Cover the dough and leave to prove for about 5 hours.
Towards the end of the 5 hours bring the oven up to baking temperature: 200°C.
Turn the batard from the proving basket onto a peel, or a flour dusted baking tray. Slash the top of the batard with a *lame* or very sharp knife.

Baking

Place the loaf in the oven and bake with steam, at 200°C, for about 1hour.

Cooling

When the loaf is removed from the oven, place it on a rack to cool.

Activity	Time	Total
Building leaven	0:05	0:05
Fermenting leaven	8:00	8:05
Building dough	0:05	8:10
Resting	0:10	8:20
Shaping	0:05	8:25
Proving	5:00	13:25
Baking	1:00	14:25
Cooling	4:00	18:25

Leaven

15g	quinoa starter
400g	water
200g	quinoa flour

Dough

615g	leaven
150g	tapioca starch
50g	quinoa flour
12g	psyllium husk
4g	salt

Additional flour for dusting the work bench and proving basket 1:1 mix of quinoa flour and tapioca starch

Buckwheat, quinoa & teff

This wholegrain loaf uses the brings out some of the best in flavour and texture from buckwheat, quinoa and teff by using a long autolysis and bassinage.

Summary
Makes: 1 loaf x 660g

Milling: buckwheat, quinoa, teff

Time to prepare: 22 ¾ hours

Baking time: 1hour

Leaven: buckwheat leaven

Leaven
This formula uses honey to increase the level of natural yeast in the buckwheat starter.

Mix 10g raw honey in 60g filtered water.
Mix 40g buckwheat starter into the honey water.
Mix 60g buckwheat flour into the starter mixture.
Set the leaven aside to ferment overnight, or for about 8 hours at around 20° C.

Dough – build 1
In a large mixing bowl mix the dry ingredients (150g buckwheat flour, 100g white quinoa flour, 50g ivory teff flour, 12g psyllium husk).
Pour 250g water onto the dry ingredients and mix well.

Autolyse
Set aside the dough to rest until the leaven is ready.

Dough – build 2
Mix the leaven into dough.
Mix in the 4g fine salt and 10g olive oil into the dough.
Knead the dough gently for about one minute.
Cover the dough and allow to stand for about 30 minutes.
Bassinage: add the additional 30g of filtered water to the dough and work it in thoroughly.

Ferment
Cover the dough and set it aside for about 8 hours to ferment.

Shaping
Prepare and dust a proving basket, preferably for a batard.
Turn the dough onto a well dusted workbench and shape before placing in the proving basket.

Proving
Cover the dough in the proving basket and set aside to prove for about 1 ½ hours.
While the dough is proving, preheat the oven to 210°C.
Prepare a peel by dusting it lightly with flour.
Turn the dough from the proving basket onto the peel.
Score the top of the loaf.

Baking
Bake at 200°C for 1 hour, with steam.

Cooling
Remove the loaf from the oven and place on a rack to cool.

Activity	Time	Total
Preparing leaven	0:05	0:05
Fermenting leaven	8:00	8:05
Dough- build 1	(0:05)	(0:10)
Autolyse	(7:50)	8:05
Dough- build 2	0:35	8:40
Fermenting	8:00	16:40
Shaping	0:05	16:45
Proving	2:00	18:45
Baking	1:00	19:45
Cooling	3:00	22:45

Leaven

40g	buckwheat starter
60g	buckwheat flour
60g	water
10g	raw honey

Dough - build 1

150g	buckwheat flour
100g	white quinoa flour
50g	ivory teff flour
12g	psyllium husk
250g	filtered water

Dough - build 2

562g	dough - build 1
170g	sweet buckwheat leaven
10g	olive oil
4g	salt, fine
30g	filtered water

Additional buckwheat flour for dusting the workbench and the proving basket

Millet sandwich loaf

Millet is a traditional food in many cultures. I grew up only knowing millet as 'bird seed'! It has a lovely mild flavour and can make delicious bread. This millet sandwich loaf requires very fine millet flour for the loaf to work properly. The formula was designed using proso millet. It will work with other millets but may require some adjustments to the hydration.

Summary

Makes: 1 loaf x 700g

Milling: millet

Time to prepare: 17 ½ hours

Baking time: 60 minutes

Leaven: millet leaven

Loaf pan size: 17cm x 10.5cm x 10.5cm

Leaven

The container used should have a capacity of 750ml to 1 litre.

Weigh 20g millet starter 40g water and 40g water into a medium mixing bowl. Mix thoroughly.
Mix 45g millet flour into the liquid,
Cover the leaven and allow to ferment for at least 4 hours.

Dough

In a large mixing bowl combine all the dry ingredients: 200g millet flour, 100g tapioca starch, 12g psyllium husk powder, and 3g salt.
Mix 270g tepid water with the leaven, then pour the leaven mixture onto the dry ingredients and combine well.
Cover the dough and set aside for about 30 minutes.
Bassinage: pour 30g tepid water onto the dough and work it in thoroughly.

Fermenting

Cover the dough and set the dough to rise for 8 hours in a warm place.

Shaping

Dust the kneading board lightly and gently knead the dough by spreading and folding it twice. Shape dough into a log and place it into a prepared loaf pan.

Proving

Cover the dough and set dough to rise in the loaf for 2 hours in a warm, draft-free place.
Preheat the oven to 220°C.

Baking

Bake at 210°C, with steam, for 60 minutes. If required return the loaf to the oven for a further 10 minutes.

Cooling

Remove the loaf from the oven, and the loaf pan, and place on a rack to cool for at least 2 hours.

Activity	Time	Total
Preparing leaven	0:05	0:05
Fermenting leaven	4:00	4:05
Building dough	0:10	4:15
Fermenting	8:00	12:15
Shaping	0:05	12:20
Proving	2:00	14:20
Baking	1:00	15:20
Cooling	2:00	17:20

Leaven

20g	millet starter
40g	water
45g	fine millet flour

Dough

105g	leaven
200g	millet flour
100g	tapioca starch
12g	psyllium husk powder
3g	salt
300g	tepid water

Kindred flax loaf

I buy my buckwheat from an organic farm at Kindred, about 20 minutes from where I live. Kindred Organics also grow quinoa and flax. In the world of bread there are many regional traditional breads that are made only from locally grown ingredients. In this loaf all ingredients for this are produced in Tasmania: buckwheat, quinoa and flax from Kindred Organics, raw honey from Tasmania's iconic forests and salt from Tasman Sea Salt.

This Kindred buckwheat and Flax loaf was probably the first purpose designed, gluten free, regional loaf!

Summary

Makes: 1 loaf x 820g

Milling: buckwheat, quinoa, flax

Hours to prepare: 18 ¼ hours

Baking time: 70 minutes

Leaven: quinoa leaven

Leaven

Place 30g quinoa starter into the bowl/jug.
Add 100g water to the starter and mix thoroughly.
Mix 100g buckwheat flour into the starter. Cover and allow the leaven to ferment for around 8 hours.

Dough - build 1

Prepare the first build of the dough as soon as the pre-ferment is covered. The long rest period for this part of the dough build is a long autolyse. This allows the flour to be thoroughly hydrated and permits the enzymes to transform starches into sugars, ready for the bacteria and yeasts in the leaven to work.

If the 300g buckwheat flour is freshly milled the 70g flax can be mixed with the buckwheat groats and the buckwheat and flax milled together.
Mix 300g buckwheat flour, 70g flax meal, and 4g salt (use a whisk to slowly mix all the dry ingredients together, ensure they are thoroughly mixed).
Mix 270g water with the dry ingredients and mix well in the bowl.
Allow the unleavened dough to stand until the leaven is ready (approximately 8 hours).

Dough - build 2

When the leaven is ready, combine dough-build 1 and 30g honey with the leaven and mix it thoroughly.

Fermenting

Cover the dough and allow to ferment for about 5 hours.

Shaping

Turn the dough onto a floured bench (buckwheat flour).
Work the dough gently by spreading and folding it twice.
Shape as a rough batard, then place the batard in a proving basket lined with a sheet of 'butter muslin' dusted with buckwheat flour.

Proving

Prove the dough for about 2 hours.
Set the oven to 220° C to preheat for at least 30 minutes.
If you are using a baking stone, allow an hour to preheat.

Baking

When the oven is ready, dust a peel with a little buckwheat flour.
Turn the dough out of the proving basket onto the peel.
Mist the top of the loaf with tepid water, then sprinkle the additional caraway seeds on the top of the loaf.
Score the top of the loaf with a sharp blade to allow the loaf to expand in the oven.
Bake at 220° C, with steam, for 20 minutes.
Reduce the temperature to 210° C and continue to bake the loaf for a further 50 minutes.

Cooling

Take the loaf from the oven and place it on a wire rack to cool.

Activity	Time	Hours
Preparing leaven	0:05	0:05
Dough - Build 1	(0:05)	0:05
Fermenting leaven	8:00	8:05
Dough - Build 2	0:05	8:10
Fermenting	3:00	11:10
Shaping	0:05	11:15
Proving	2:00	13:15
Baking	1:00	14:15
Cooling	4:00	18:15

Leaven

30g	quinoa starter
100g	water
100g	buckwheat flour

Dough

230g	buckwheat leaven
300g	buckwheat flour
70g	flax meal
4g	salt
270g	water
30g	raw honey

Buckwheat & chestnut bread

Chestnuts are a versatile seed that can be used to make flour for use in cooking and baking. After a number of years trying to find chestnut flour I found some fresh chestnuts one Autumn and set about making the flour myself.

Chestnut flour works beautifully with buckwheat flour to make this delicious and nutritious sourdough bread.

See notes on making chestnut flour on page 16.

Summary

Makes: 1 loaf x720g

Milling: buckwheat, quinoa, chestnut

Hours to prepare: 20 ¼ hours

Baking time: 1 hour

Leaven: quinoa leaven + buckwheat leaven

Leaven

This formula uses two separate leavens. Each leaven is developed separately. The two leavens are only brought together in the final dough.

Prepare 50g quinoa leaven by mixing the ingredients in a small bowl.
Prepare 50g buckwheat leaven by mixing the ingredients in a separate small bowl.

Dough

In a large mixing bowl mix the dry ingredients: 225g buckwheat flour, 75g chestnut flour, 12g psyllium husk, and 6g salt.
In a medium bowl mix 300g water, 50g quinoa leaven, and 50g buckwheat leaven.
Pour the water and leaven mixture onto the dry ingredients mix and combine thoroughly into a smooth dough.
Knead the dough gently for about one minute.
Cover the dough and allow to stand for about 30 minutes.
Bassinage: add 30 g of filtered water to the dough and work it in thoroughly.

Fermenting

Cover the dough and set it aside for the bulk ferment for about 7 hours.

Shaping

Prepare and dust a proving basket.
Turn the dough onto a well dusted workbench and shape before placing in the proving basket.

Proving

Cover the dough in the proving basket and set aside to prove.
While the dough is proving, preheat the oven to 210°C.

Baking

Prepare a peel by dusting it lightly with flour.
Turn the dough from the proving basket onto the peel.
Score the top of the loaf.
Bake with steam, at 200°C ,for one hour.

Cooling

Remove the loaf from the oven and place it on a rack to cool for at least 3 hours. This loaf is better if not cut for 24 hours after baking.

Activity	Time	Total
Preparing leavens	0:05	0:05
Fermenting leavens	8:00	8:05
Building dough	0:35	8:40
Fermenting	7:00	15:40
Shaping	0:05	15:45
Proving	1:30	17:15
Baking	1:00	18:15
Cooling	3:00	21:15

Leavens

10g	quinoa starter
20g	water
20g	quinoa flour
10g	buckwheat starter
20g	water
20g	buckwheat flour

Dough

50g	quinoa leaven
50g	buckwheat leaven
225g	buckwheat flour
75g	chestnut flour
12g	psyllium husk
6g	salt
330 g	filtered water

Additional buckwheat flour for dusting the workbench and the proving basket

Promise & Fulfilment - real bread without gluten

Buckwheat pumpernickel

Buckwheat pumpernickel draws on the tradition of eastern European cracked rye breads to produce a flavoursome, moist bread that is sliced thinly for open sandwiches.

This formula requires a closed roasting or baking pan with water approximately 2cm deep in the lower part of the baking pan. The loaf pan is placed in the lower part of the baking pan, and the lid is placed onto the baking pan during most of the bake.

Summary

Makes: 1 loaf x 660g

Milling: buckwheat

Hours to prepare: 44 ½ hours

Baking time: 4 hours

Leaven: buckwheat leaven

Country loaf pan 17.5 x 12 x 7 cm

Soaker

The longest activity in this formula is 'Fermenting Soaker'. Other activities: 'Preparing scald', and 'prepare leaven' are done during the 'Fermenting soaker' time so that when the soaker is ready, the scald and leaven are also ready to use in building the dough.

Weigh 250g cracked buckwheat groats, 2g cracked caraway seed, and 1g cracked fennel seed into a large mixing bowl. Add 230g water a little at a time, mix thoroughly.
Cover the soaker and set it aside to ferment for 24 hours.

Scald/Malt

Weigh 30g cracked buckwheat groats, and 5g buckwheat diastatic malt flour into a glass or ceramic lidded jar.
Add 150g hot water, 70°C, a little at a time, initially create a paste, then gradually dilute the paste until all the hot water has been added.
Cover the scald and keep it at approximately 70°C until the leaven is ready. Keep at 70°C. See page 42 for notes on malting.

Leaven

Prepare 50g buckwheat leaven by mixing the ingredients in a small bowl.
Cover the leaven and set it aside to ferment for 8 hours.

Dough

In a large mixing bowl mix the scald and the soaker together.
Mix leaven into the soaker & scald mixture to form dough.
Add 5g fine sea salt to the dough.
Mix well in the bowl; you should have soft, sticky dough.

Shaping

Spoon the dough into a well greased loaf pan.

Fermenting

Cover the dough and set it to rise overnight, or for about 8 hours, in a warm, draft free place.
Preheat the oven to 230° C

Baking

Bake in a hot oven using the following temperature and timing schedule:
(4 hours total baking time):

230° C for 30 minutes, then
200° C for 30 minutes,
180° C for 30 minutes,
160° C for 30 minutes,
140° C for 30 minutes,
120° C for 30 minutes,
110° C for 30 minutes,
100° C for 30 minutes.

Cooling

Remove loaf pan from the closed baking pan, then remove the loaf and place it on a rack to cool – allow 4 hours for cooling. It is better not to slice this loaf until 24 hours after baking.

Activity	Time	Total
Preparing Soaker	0:05	0:05
Fermenting Soaker	24:00	24:05
Preparing scald	(0:05)	24:05
Malting scald	(23:50)	24:05
Preparing leaven	(0:05)	24:05
Fermenting Leaven	(8:00)	24:05
Building Dough	0:05	24:10
Fermenting	8:00	32:10
Baking	4:00	36:10
Cooling	4:00	44:10

Scald

30g	buckwheat flour
5g	buckwheat diastatic malt flour
150g	hot water, 70°C

Leavens

10g	buckwheat starter
20g	water
20g	buckwheat flour

Soaker

250g	buckwheat groats, cracked
2g	caraway seed, cracked
1g	fennel seed, cracked
230g	water

Dough

50g	buckwheat leaven
180g	buckwheat scald
480g	soaker
5g	fine sea salt

Promise & Fulfilment - real bread without gluten

Quinoa, sweet rice & buckwheat loaf

This loaf highlights the flexibility and richness of quinoa, sweet rice, and buckwheat. Together with the buckwheat starter, a small amount of bee barm (honey yeast water) is used to provide a richly flavoured bread with a sweetness that comes from the flours, not the bee barm. The bee barm is fermented and the sugars from the honey are consumed during fermentation.

Use white, red, or black quinoa and white, black, or purple sweet rice to design a lightly coloured, or robust dark loaf.

See page 29 for information about preparing bee barm (honey yeast water).

See page 42 for information about preparing buckwheat diastatic malt flour.

Summary

Makes: 1 x 600g loaf

Milling: buckwheat, sweet rice, quinoa

Hours to prepare: 23 ½ hours

Baking time: 70 minutes

Leaven: buckwheat leaven + honey yeast water

Leaven

In a large mixing bowl mix 30g buckwheat starter in 150g of water.
Mix 150g of freshly milled buckwheat flour into the starter liquid.
Add 10g of bee barm to the leaven and mix thoroughly.
Cover the leaven and set aside for 8 hours to ferment.

Dough

In a medium mixing bowl mix 75g sweet rice flour, 75g quinoa flour, 12g psyllium husk, 4g buckwheat diastatic malt flour, and 3g salt.
Mix 130g of water into the leaven.
Mix the dry ingredients into the liquid leaven.

Fermenting

Cover the dough and allow to ferment for about 8 hours.

Shaping

Turn the dough onto a lightly floured bench.
Work the dough gently by spreading and folding it twice.
Shape the dough into a batard.

Proving

Place the dough into a suitable banneton. Cover and allow to rise for about an hour. Preheat the oven to 230°C.

Baking

When the oven is up to temperature place a metal dish with boiling water into the oven on a shelf below the shelf on which the loaf will be baked.

Score the loaf.
Bake at 220°C with steam for 20 minutes. Reduce the temperature to 210°C and continue to bake for a further 50 minutes.

Cooling

Remove the loaf from the oven and place on a rack to cool.

Activity	Time	Total
Preparing leaven	0:05	0:05
Fermenting leaven	8:00	8:05
Building dough	0:05	8:10
Fermenting	8:00	16:10
Shaping	0:05	16:15
Proving	1:00	17:15
Baking	0:70	19:25
Cooling	4:00	23:25

Leaven

30g	buckwheat starter
10g	bee barm
150g	water
150g	buckwheat flour

Dough

340g	buckwheat leaven
75g	sweet rice flour
75g	quinoa flour
12g	psyllium husk
4g	buckwheat diastatic malt flour
3g	salt
130g	water

Baguette formulas

Amaranth baguettes

One of the challenges of bread baking is the baguette. The crisp crust and soft open crumb seem to rely heavily on the presence of gluten. So, for many years baking a good baguette became a challenge. Baking with amaranth flour, particularly with sourdough provides another set of challenges. The amaranth baguette provides a crisp crust, a soft, open crumb and a rich complex flavour that rewards the effort spent in preparing, fermenting and baking.

Summary

Makes: 3 x 200g baguettes

Milling: brown rice, amaranth

Hours to prepare: 46 ¼ hours

Baking time: 45 minutes

Leaven: brown rice leaven

Leaven

Prepare 50g brown rice leaven by mixing the ingredients in a small bowl.
Cover the leaven and ferment for 8 hours.

Dough – build 1

Mix 50g leaven in 330g water in a large mixing bowl.
Mix 150g tapioca flour and 50g amaranth flour into the liquid.

Fermenting

Cover & set aside for 1 hour.
Place dough in refrigerator overnight (8 to 10 hrs).

Dough – build 2

Remove the dough from the refrigerator and rest it at room temperature.
In a small bowl mix the remaining flour: 50g amaranth flour and 50g tapioca starch with 12g psyllium husk and 3g salt.
Mix the dry ingredients thoroughly into the dough.

Fermenting

Cover & set aside for 1 hour.
Place dough in refrigerator for 24 hours (up to 36 hrs).
Remove dough from refrigerator and rest it at room temperature for an hour.

Shaping

Remove dough from bowl, to a lightly dusted work bench.
Dust the workbench lightly with tapioca starch.
Gently work the dough.
The dough may seem solid and difficult to work, just be gentle and it will yield.

Divide dough into 3 lumps (about 215g each).
Shape each piece of dough as short finger bun.
Set each pre-shaped bun on a dusted portion of the bench, or a tray. Cover the dough and rest for about 1 hour.
Taking the pre-shaped dough one by one, roll each one gently on the bench, drawing it out towards a baguette shape.
As each baguette is rolled out pause, and with a thumb press a line down the centre of the baguette.
Fold the baguette along the line and continue gently rolling the baguette.
When the desired length and diameter is achieved place the baguette seam side up on a couche.

Proving

When all three baguettes are in the folded couche, cover the baguettes and set aside to prove for about 1 hour.
Preheat the oven to 220°C.

Baking

Place the baguettes seam side down on a peel, or baguette tray.
Prepare a steam dish for the oven.
Score each baguette.
Place the baguettes in the oven on an oven stone.
Bake at 200°C for 45 minutes.

Cooling

Remove baguettes from the oven and place on a rack to cool.

Activity	Time	Total
Preparing leaven	0:05	0:05
Fermenting leaven	8:00	8:05
Build dough 1	0:05	8:10
Fermenting dough	9:00	17:10
Build dough 2	0:05	17:15
Fermenting	26:00	43:15
Shaping	0:40	43:55
Proving	1:00	44:55
Baking	0:45	45:40
Cooling	0:30	46:10

Leavens

10g	brown rice starter
20g	water
20g	brown rice flour

Dough - build 1

50 g	brown rice leaven
50 g	amaranth flour
150 g	tapioca starch
330 g	water

Dough - build 2

580g	dough - build 1
50 g	amaranth flour
50 g	tapioca starch
12 g	psyllium husk
3 g	salt

Buckwheat & chestnut baguettes

The challenge of making baguettes can become intoxicating. Having made one good baguette, and then another, and then another the question always remains: 'Can I make a better baguette?'

The buckwheat and chestnut baguette with its crisp crust and soft, open crumb, with complex and sweet flavours from the chestnut and buckwheat is just another attempt at answering the question.

See notes on making chestnut flour on page 16.

Summary

Makes: 3 baguettes 180g each

Milling: brown rice, buckwheat, chestnut

Hours to prepare: 20 ¼ hours

Baking time: 40 minutes

Leaven: brown rice leaven + buckwheat leaven

Leaven

This formula uses two separate leavens. Each leaven is prepared separately. The two leavens are only brought together in the final dough.

Prepare 50g brown rice leaven and 50g buckwheat leaven by mixing the ingredients for each in a separate small bowl. Cover the leavens and set aside for 8 hours to ferment.

Dough

In a medium bowl mix 50g brown rice leaven and 50g buckwheat leaven with 300g of water.
In the large bowl put all the dry ingredients: 75g buckwheat flour, 75g chestnut flour, 150g tapioca starch, 12g psyllium husk, and 5g salt. Mix the dry ingredients thoroughly.
Pour the water and leaven mix onto the dry ingredients and mix them thoroughly. Cover and set the dough aside to rest for about 15 minutes.
Bassinage: add the remaining 30g water to the dough and work it in thoroughly.

Fermenting

Cover the dough and allow it to rest for about 1 hour, then place in the refrigerator for at least 8 hours, and up to 36 hours. Remove dough from bowl, to a lightly dusted work bench.

Shaping

Dust the workbench lightly with tapioca starch, or buckwheat flour.
Divide the dough into 3 equal portions; approximately 230 g each.
Taking the lumps of dough one by one, gently flatten and shape each piece to a rough square.
Roll each one gently on the bench, drawing it out towards a baguette shape. When the desired length and diameter is achieved put the baguette seam side up on a couche (be sure that the baguette will fit in the oven!)

Proving

When all three baguettes are in the folded couche, cover the baguettes and set aside to prove for about 1 ½ hours.
Preheat the oven to 220°C before the end of the proving time.

Baking

Place the baguettes seam side down on a peel, or baguette tray.
Prepare a steam dish for the oven.
Score each baguette.
Place the baguettes in the oven on an oven stone.
Bake at 200°C for 40 minutes.

Cooling

Remove baguettes from the oven and place on a rack to cool.

Activity	Time	Total
Preparing leavens	0:05	0:05
Fermenting leavens	8:00	8:05
Building dough	0:35	8:40
Fermenting	9:00	17:40
Shaping	0:05	17:45
Proving	1:30	19:15
Baking	0:40	19:55
Cooling	0:15	20:10

Leavens

10g	brown rice starter
20g	water
20g	brown rice flour
10g	buckwheat starter
20g	water
20g	buckwheat flour

Dough

50g	brown rice leaven
50g	buckwheat leaven
75g	buckwheat flour
75g	chestnut flour
150g	tapioca starch
12g	psyllium husk
5g	salt
330g	water

Rice baguettes

Rice baguettes are delicious: a crisp crust and soft crumb.

The range of rice varieties is vast, so the possibilities for rice baguettes is enormous. Sweet or sticky rice should not be used in this formula, but that is the only caution. Even using brown rice and black rice in different ratios can yield a range of very different baguettes from straight brown through shades of pastel pink to vibrant purple. In a similar way the choice of rice will provide different flavours from a smoky black rice to the sweetness of jasmine rice, or the nuttiness of aged brown basmati rice.

Leaven

Prepare 50g brown rice leaven by mixing the ingredients in a small bowl.
Cover the leaven and set aside to ferment for 8 hours.

Pre-ferment

The rice flour used in the pre-ferment can give different characteristics to the dough and final baguettes. A mixture of white, black, red, or brown rice flour can be used to vary the colour. It is better to use no more than 50g black rice flour or sweet rice flour in the mixture. Jasmine or another aromatic rice flour can also be used to vary the flavour.

Put 50g brown rice leaven in large mixing bowl.
Add 250g of water to the leaven and stir it thoroughly.
Add 150g rice flour to the leaven mix.
Cover the pre-ferment and allow it to rest for approximately 8 hours.

Dough

In a small bowl mix the dry ingredients: 150g tapioca starch, and 15g psyllium husk and 3g salt.
Add the dry ingredients to the pre-ferment and mix thoroughly.
Cover and set the dough aside to rest for about 20 minutes.
Bassinage: add the remaining 50g water to the dough and work it in thoroughly.

Fermenting

Cover the dough and allow it to rest for approximately 8 hours.

Shaping

Remove dough from bowl, to a lightly dusted work bench.
Dust the workbench lightly with tapioca starch, or fine rice flour.
Divide the dough into 3 equal portions; approximately 220g each.
Shape each piece of dough as short log.
Set the shaped dough on a dusted portion of the bench.
Taking the pre-shaped dough one by one, roll each one gently on the bench, drawing it out towards a baguette shape.
As each baguette is rolled out pause, and with a thumb press a line down the centre of the baguette.
Fold the baguette along the line and continue gently rolling the baguette.
When the desired length and diameter is achieved put the baguette seam side up on a couche.

Proving

When all three baguettes are in the folded couche, cover the baguettes and set aside to rise for about 1 hour.
Preheat the oven to 220°C.

Baking

Place the baguettes seam side down on a peel, or baguette tray.
Prepare a steam dish for the oven.
Score each baguette.
Place the baguettes in the oven on an oven stone.
Bake at 200°C for 40 minutes.

Cooling

Remove baguettes from the oven and place on a rack to cool.

Summary

Makes: 3 baguettes 225g each

Milling: brown rice, plus rice of your choice

Hours to prepare: 26 hours

Baking time: 40 minutes

Leaven: brown rice leaven

Activity	Time	Total
Preparing leaven	0:05	0:05
Fermenting leaven	8:00	8:05
Preparing pre-ferment	0:05	8:10
Fermenting pre-ferment	8:00	16:10
Building dough	0:25	16:35
Fermenting	8:00	24:35
Shaping	0:05	24:40
Proving	1:00	25:40
Baking	0:40	26:20
Cooling	0:15	26:35

Leaven

10g	brown rice starter
20g	water
20g	brown rice flour

Pre-ferment

50g	brown rice leaven
150g	rice flour
250g	water

Dough

450g	pre-ferment
150g	tapioca starch
15g	psyllium husk
3g	salt
50g	water

Millet baguettes

Millet can be a lovely flour if it is finely milled, and fresh. Millet baguettes are always a treat. They pair readily with so many good foods.

Summary

Makes: 3 baguettes x 150g each

Milling: millet

Hours to prepare: 19 ¼ hours

Baking time: 45 minutes

Leaven: millet leaven

Leaven

Prepare 50g millet leaven by mixing the ingredients in a small bowl.

Cover the leaven and set aside to ferment for 8 hours.

Dough

In a large mixing bowl mix the dry ingredients: 150g millet flour, 150g tapioca starch, 12g psyllium husk and 3g salt.

Mix the dry ingredients thoroughly.

Mix 260g tepid water with the leaven.

Add the leaven mixture and 5g olive oil to the dry ingredients and mix thoroughly.

Cover the dough and set aside for 15 minutes.

Bassinage: add the remaining 30g water to the dough and mix in thoroughly.

Fermenting

Cover the dough and allow it to rest for approximately 8 hours.

Shaping

Remove dough from bowl, to a lightly dusted work bench.

Dust the workbench lightly with tapioca starch.

Work the dough gently by spreading and folding it twice.

Divide the dough into 3 equal portions; approximately 215g each.

Shape each piece of dough as short finger bun.

Set each pre-shaped bun on a dusted portion of the bench, or a tray.

Cover the dough and rest for about 30 minutes.

Taking the pre-shaped dough one by one, roll each one gently on the bench, drawing it out towards a baguette shape.

As each baguette is rolled out pause, and with a thumb press a line down the centre of the baguette.

Fold the baguette along the line and continue gently rolling the baguette.

When the desired length and diameter is achieved put the baguette seam side up on a couche.

Proving

When all three baguettes are in the folded couche, cover the baguettes and set aside to prove for about 1 hour.

Preheat the oven to 220°C.

Baking

Place the baguettes seam side down on a peel, or baguette tray.

Prepare a steam dish for the oven.

Score each baguette.

Place the baguettes in the oven on an oven stone.

Bake, with steam, at 200°C for 45 minutes.

Cooling

Remove baguettes from the oven and place on a rack to cool.

Activity	Time	Total
Preparing leaven	0:05	0:05
Fermenting leaven	8:00	8:05
Building dough	0:05	8:35
Fermenting	8:00	16:35
Shaping	0:40	17:15
Proving	1:00	18:15
Baking	0:45	19:00
Cooling	0:15	19:15

Leaven

10g	millet starter
20g	water
20g	millet flour

Dough

50g	millet leaven
150g	millet flour
150g	tapioca starch
12g	psyllium husk
3g	salt
5g	olive oil
290g	tepid water

Flatbread formulas

Millet focaccia

Golden millet freshly milled into fine flour is the basis of this Millet Focaccia. Drizzled with olive oil, and topped with fresh rosemary and a little sea salt, it can be served as a simple meal or as part of a larger meal.

Summary

Makes: 1 focaccia x 630g

Milling: millet

Hours to prepare: 11 hours

Baking time: 25 minutes

Leaven: millet leaven

Leaven

In a medium bowl mix 100g water and 10g millet starter, and 100g millet flour.
Cover the bowl and allow the mixture to ferment for around eight hours.

Dough

In a large bowl mix the dry ingredients: 100g millet flour, 100g tapioca starch, 12g psyllium husk, and 3g salt, Do this gently to ensure all the ingredients are well combined.
Mix 200g tepid water with the dry ingredients.
Combine the leaven with the dough and mix until the dough comes away from the bowl.
Add 20g olive oil to the dough.
Mix well in the bowl.

Fermenting

Set dough aside for 15 minutes to rest. Turn dough out onto the workbench, and knead for a few minutes by gently spreading and folding the dough twice.

Shaping

Shape dough into a 20 cm to 25 cm disk and place on an oiled baking sheet, cover shaped dough.

Proving

Set dough to rise for about 2 hours in a warm, draft-free place.
Preheat the oven to 220°C for at least 30 minutes.

Dressing

Brush additional olive oil across the top of the focaccia, then sprinkle with salt and herbs or olive slices before putting in the oven.
Using your fingertips press the salt and rosemary leaves into the top of the dough.

Baking

Bake at 210°C for 20 - 25 minutes.

Cooling

Allow the focaccia to cool for 10 to 15 minutes before serving while still warm.

Variation

This variation allows the Millet Focaccia to be leavened with bakers' yeast, either instant yeast or fresh yeast.

In a medium bowl mix 100g water and 1g yeast, and 100g millet flour.
For fresh yeast use tepid water. Allow the yeast to stand for a few minutes before adding the millet flour.

Cover the bowl or jug and allow the mixture to ferment for around eight hours.

Leaven

1g	instant yeast
(2g)	(fresh yeast)
100g	water
100g	fine millet flour

Activity	Time	Total
Preparing leaven	0:05	0:05
Fermenting leaven	8:00	8:05
Building dough	0:10	8:15
Fermenting	0:15	8:30
Shaping	0:03	8:33
Proving	2:00	10:33
Dressing	0:07	10:40
Baking	0:25	11:05
Cooling	0:10	11:15

Leaven

10g	millet starter
100g	millet flour
100g	water

Dough

210g (201g)	millet leaven
100g	millet flour
100g	tapioca starch
12g	psyllium husk
3g	salt
20g	olive oil
200g	tepid water

Topping

3g	salt
10g	olive oil
15g	fresh rosemary leaves

Olive fougasse

Fougasse can be prepared with olives, or any preferred fruit or vegetable: fresh or preserved.

This can be prepared with instant dried yeast, or with sourdough: see the variation for instant dried yeast.

Summary

Makes: 3 fougasse approximately 300g

Milling: millet, arborio rice

Hours to prepare: 12 ½ hours

Baking time: 25 minutes

Leaven: millet leaven, or brown rice leaven, or instant dried yeast

Leaven

Prepare 250g millet leaven by mixing the ingredients in a medium bowl.
Cover the bowl and allow the mixture to ferment for around 8 hours.

Dough – build 1

This can be prepared after the leaven and allowed to rest while the leaven ferments.
In a large mixing bowl mix the dry ingredients (100g millet flour, 100g arborio rice flour, 12g psyllium husk powder, 4 g salt)
Mix 250g tepid water with the dry ingredients.
Cover and set aside to rest for at least 30 minutes before the next stage of building the dough.

Dough – build 2

Combine the leaven with dough build 1.
Add 25g olive oil to the dough and mix it in thoroughly.
Take the 30g olives and gently fold them into the dough a few at a time.

Fermenting

Set dough to rise for 1 ½ hours in a warm, draft free place.

Shaping

Divide dough into 3 pieces approximately 260g each.
Gently form a ball with each piece, then gently flatten it to approximately 1.5cm thick.
Using a dough scraper cut 1 slot down the centre and 4 angled slots down each side of the round to make the leaf pattern.
Repeat for each piece.

Place each shaped fougasse on a lined baking sheet and cover.

Proving

Set dough to rise for about 1 ½ hours in a warm, draft-free place.
Preheat the oven to 210°C.

Baking

Bake in a hot oven at 200°C for 25 minutes.

Cooling

Remove fougasse from the oven and place on a rack to cool for a few minutes before serving.

Variation

Leaven – pre-ferment

1g	instant dried yeast
125g	millet flour
125g	water

In a medium bowl mix the 1g instant dried yeast and 125g water.
Mix 125g millet flour into liquid.
Cover the bowl and allow the mixture to ferment for around 8 hours.

Activity	Time	Total
Preparing leaven	0:05	0:05
Fermenting leaven	8:00	8:05
Dough – build 1	0:05	8:10
Resting dough	(8:00)	8:10
Dough – build 2	0:35	8:45
Fermenting	1:30	10:15
Shaping	0:05	10:20
Proving	1:30	11:50
Baking	0:25	12:15
Cooling	0:10	12:25

Leaven

50g	millet starter
100g	water
100g	millet flour

Dough – build 1

100g	millet flour
100g	arborio rice flour
12g	psyllium husk powder
4g	salt
250g	tepid water

Dough – build 2

250g	millet leaven
466g	dough – build 1
30g	olives, pitted, sliced, and drained
25g	olive oil

Pita

Millet, a traditional food in many cultures, is an ancient grain that has been used as a staple food for centuries. Millet may have been one of the seeds used in the original pitas or flat breads.

There are many different millets, see page 17 for more information about millet. The millet used in this pita is proso millet (panicum miliaceum).

Summary

Makes: 4 pitas, 17cm diameter

Milling: millet, sweet rice

Hours to prepare: 11 ½ hours

Baking time: 5 minutes each batch

Leaven: millet leaven

Leaven

Prepare 100g millet leaven.
In a small bowl mix the leaven ingredients. Cover the leaven and allow to ferment for at least 4 hours.

Scald

In a large mixing bowl combine 150g millet flour and 100g tapioca starch.
Pour 200g boiling water onto the flour mixture and, using a mixing spoon or dough whisk, mix well.
Cover and set aside to cool to 40°C.

Dough

In a small mixing bowl combine the remaining dry ingredients: 50g sweet rice flour, 15g psyllium husk powder, and 3g salt.
Mix the leaven in to the scald.
Mix the dry ingredients into the scald.
Add 10g olive oil to the dough and work it in thoroughly.

Fermenting

Cover the dough and set the dough to ferment for 1 hour in a warm place.
Dust the workbench lightly and gently knead the dough by spreading and folding it 4 times.
Roll the dough into a ball.
Cover the dough and allow it to continue fermenting for another 5 hours.

Shaping

Divide the dough into 4 equal pieces. Dust the work bench, then roll each piece into a ball, then gradually work it into a disk 5cm thick.
The thickness is important: if it is too thick or too thin, the pita will not inflate.

Proving

Cover the dough and set dough to rise in the loaf for 30 minutes in a warm, draft-free place.
With an oven stone in place, preheat the oven to 230°C, or as hot as you can safely manage.

Baking

Lightly dust each round.
Place each round on the baking stone to bake, turning after about 2 minutes.
As each pita expands allow it to bake a few more minutes. The total baking time is about 5 minutes

Cooling

Remove the pita from the oven and place on a rack to cool.

Activity	Time	Total
Preparing leaven	0:05	0:05
Fermenting leaven	4:00	4:05
Building dough	0:45	4:50
Fermenting	6:00	10:50
Shaping	0:05	10:55
Proving	0:30	11:25
Baking	0:05	11:30
Cooling	0:05	11:35

Leaven

20g	millet starter
40g	water
40g	millet flour

Scald

150g	millet flour
100g	tapioca starch
200g	water, boiling

Dough

100g	millet leaven
50g	sweet rice flour
15g	psyllium husk powder
3g	salt
10g	olive oil

Where bases are to be frozen:

If the pizza base is to be frozen, bake on a lined baking sheet, in a hot oven 230°C. Allow 10 minutes for each batch to be part baked. Allow the base to cool before wrapping and freezing.

For the best results for bases that are to be frozen, mark the dough base with a pastry docking tool before baking.

Lining the sheet with baking paper is recommended for bases that are to be part baked, and then frozen. The base can be frozen on the baking paper.

Where a wood fired pizza oven is to be used:

If baking in a woodfired oven the temperatures will be much higher, so the baking time will be between 1 and 10 minutes.

DO NOT bake the pizza on baking paper in a wood fired oven!

Use a peel onto to place the pizza on the the floor of the oven. Recover the pizza from the oven with the peel. Or:

Prepare the pizza on a metal pizza tray, using a peel to place the tray on the floor of the oven, and recover the pizza.

Pizza

Pizza is one of those foods that we all enjoy but take a little for granted until it is off our menu. Getting a slice of pizza that is safe to eat can return to us the joy of sharing food!

Pizza bases can be par-baked and frozen for later use.

This dough can be made with lievito madre *(my preferred method) or with a stiff brown rice starter if* lievito madre *is not available.*

Summary

Makes: 4 x pizzas 25cm

Hours to prepare: 9 ½ hours

Baking time:15-20 minutes each – depending on topping (10 minutes for par-bake before freezing)

Leaven options: *lievito madre,* or brown rice leaven

Leaven

Prepare 200g *lievito madre*. See page 35.

Dough

In a medium jug or mixing bowl mix 370g tepid water with 200g *lievito madre*.
In a large mixing bowl combine all the dry ingredients: 150g millet flour, 150g brown rice flour, 150g tapioca starch, 15g psyllium husk powder, 6g salt.
Pour the leaven mixture onto the dry ingredients and combine well.
Cover the dough and set aside for about 15 minutes.
Pour 65g tepid water onto the dough and work it in thoroughly.
Mix 30g olive oil to the dough and work it in thoroughly.

Fermenting

Cover the dough and set the dough to rise for 2 hours in a warm place.
Gently spread and fold the dough twice.
Cover the dough and rest for 1 hour.

Shaping

Dust the kneading board lightly and gently knead the dough by spreading and folding it twice.
Divide the dough into 4 equal pieces.
Rest the dough for 30 minutes.
Roll each piece into a ball, then gradually work it into a flat disk about 25 cm in diameter.

Proving

Preheat the oven to 230ºC.
Place the pizza base on a lined oven sheet or pizza tray.
Cover the bases and set to rise for 1 hour in a warm, draft-free place.
If the pizza base is to be used immediately, top the pizza as desired.

Baking

Bake in a hot oven 230ºC for 15-20 minutes.
Remove from the oven, cut into segments and serve.

Variation - leaven

In a medium mixing bowl mix 20g brown rice starter with 60g water.
Add 120g brown rice flour into the mixture and combine well. Cover the leaven and set aside to ferment for 8 hours.
Add 4 hours to 'Fermenting leaven' in the schedule when this variation is used.

Leaven - pre-ferment

20g	brown rice starter
60g	water
120g	brown rice flour

Activity	Time	Total
Preparing leaven	0:05	0:05
Fermenting leaven	4:00	4:05
Building dough	0:20	4:25
Fermenting	3:00	7:25
Shaping	0:35	8:00
Prove	1:00	9:00
Baking	0:20	9:20
Bake (for bases to freeze)	(0:10)	(9:10)
Cooling (for bases to freeze)	(0:30)	(9:40)

Dough

200g	leaven
150g	brown rice flour
150g	millet flour
150g	tapioca starch
15g	psyllium husk powder
6g	salt
435g	tepid water
30g	olive oil

Rice & chia wraps

Wraps are useful for food on the go and for school lunches. These wraps are soft and pliable, working well with a range of fillings.

They can be stored for use the next day, or frozen. Warm wraps gently before use if they have been frozen or if they are more than a day old.

Wraps can also be used as a thin base for pizza: brush the wrap with olive oil and top before baking the pizza.

These wraps are cooked in a 4-slice sandwich press.

There are two batches of wraps shown in the photograph. One batch was made with sourdough and black sweet rice, the other was made with white sweet rice and yeast.

Summary

Makes: 4 wraps

Milling: brown rice, sweet rice

Hours to prepare: 3 ½ hours

Cooking time: 10 minutes

Leaven: brown rice starter

Leaven

Prepare 100g brown rice leaven.
In a small bowl mix the leaven ingredients.
Cover the leaven and allow to ferment for 2 hours.

Dough

Chia seed can be milled if you prefer a smooth wrap rather than a seeded wrap.

Mix 5g oil and 100g tepid water into the leaven.
In a medium mixing bowl mix all dry ingredients: 50g brown rice flour, 50g sweet rice flour, 20g chia seed, 5g psyllium husk, and 3g fine salt.
Mix well in the bowl.

Fermenting

Set dough to rise for 30 minutes in a warm place, until about double its original size.
Knead gently for a few minutes.
A little extra flour during kneading to dust the work bench and dough.

Shaping

Divide the dough into 4 pieces (about 80g each).
Shape each piece of dough into a flat disk about 10 cm in diameter, and place on a lightly floured baking sheet.

Proving

Set the dough round to rise for 30 minutes in a warm place.
Preheat the sandwich press.
Roll each dough round with a rolling pin, or press out by hand until the dough round is about 20 cm in diameter and about 1mm to 1.5mm thick.
Dust each round lightly with either fine rice flour or tapioca starch and allow them to rest for a few minutes.

Cooking

One at a time, cook the rounds in the sandwich press. Check the round after 1 minute: maximum cooking time should be about 1 ½ minutes for each wrap.
A little browning of the wrap is alright.
Too much browning will crisp the crust.

Lay the wraps on a rack to cool and cover them to retain moisture.
If wraps feel too crisp, allow them to rest longer.

The wraps will all soften as the moisture inside the wrap evens out through the wrap.

Variation - leaven

In a small mixing bowl mix 0.5g instant dried yeast and 50g rice flour.
Mix 50g tepid water into the flour & yeast mixture.
Set side and allow to ferment for 2 hours.

50g	rice flour (white or brown)
50g	tepid water
0.5g	instant dried yeast

Activity	Time	Total
Preparing leaven	0:05	0:05
Fermenting leaven	1:00	1:05
Building dough	0:05	1:10
Fermenting	0:30	1:40
Shaping	0:05	1:45
Proving	0:30	2:45
Cooking	0:10	2:55
Cooling	0:30	3:25

Leaven

20g	brown rice starter
40g	water
40g	brown rice flour

Dough

100g	leaven
50g	brown rice flour
50g	sweet rice flour
20g	chia seed
5g	psyllium husks
3g	fine salt
5g	light cooking oil
100g	tepid water

Seeded bread formulas

Sunshine loaf

Seeded loaves are always delicious especially when the seed is toasted before it is mixed in the dough. This Sunshine Loaf brings together the wholesome flavours of brown rice, golden millet, flaxseeds, and sunflower seeds. The techniques are a little more challenging but are well rewarded.

Leaven

This formula uses two separate leavens. Each leaven is developed separately. The two leavens are only brought together in the final dough.

Prepare 50g millet leaven and 50g brown rice leaven by mixing the the ingredients for each in separate small bowls.
Cover the leavens and set aside to ferment for about 8 hours.

Toasting

Toast 30g flax seeds and 50g hulled sunflower seeds. Set seeds aside to cool.

Dough – scald

Put 150g brown rice flour and 50g millet flour in a large mixing bowl.
Add 200g hot water into the flour mix.
Allow the flour mix to cool.
Check the temperature flour & water mixture in the large mixing bowl.
When the temperature is at or below 40°C commence the next stage.

Dough – final

Mix the remaining dry ingredients: 100g millet flour, 10g psyllium husk and 5g salt in a small bowl.
Pour the 50g millet leaven, 50g brown rice leaven and 100g water (room temperature) in a separate bowl.
Pour the leaven mixture into the large mixing bowl with the scalded dough and mix it in thoroughly.
Add the mixed dry ingredients to the wet ingredients in the large mixing bowl.
Add the toasted seeds to the large mixing bowl.
Mix all the ingredients thoroughly in the large mixing bowl.
Bassinage: allow the dough to stand for 30 minutes.
Add the remaining 30g of water, mixing it thoroughly with the dough.

Fermenting

Cover the dough and set aside to ferment in a warm place for about six hours.

Shaping

Turn the dough onto a lightly dusted workbench, and gently work it into a disc of around 15 cm in diameter and 2 ½ cm thick.
Gently roll the disc of dough to form a batard shape and place it seam upwards in a proving basket.

Proving

Cover the dough and set the dough aside in a warm place for about one hour.
Preheat the oven to 220°C.

Baking

Bake, with steam, at 210ºC for 60 minutes.

Cooling

Remove the loaf from the oven and place on a rack to cool. Allow at least 3 hours to cool.

Summary

Makes: 1 loaf x 800g

Milling: millet, brown rice

Hours to prepare: 15 ½ hours

Baking time: 1 hour

Leaven: millet starter + brown rice starter

Activity	Time	Total
Preparing leaven	0:05	0:05
Fermenting leaven	4: 00	4: 05
Toasting	0:05	4:10
Dough - scald	0:05	4:45
Dough - final	0:35	5:20
Fermenting	6:00	11:20
Shaping	0:05	11:25
Baking	1:00	12:25
Cooling	3:00	15:25

Leavens

10g	millet starter
20g	water
20g	millet flour
10g	brown rice starter
20g	water
20g	brown rice flour

Toasting

30g	flax seed
50g	sunflower seed, hulled

Scald

150g	brown rice flour
50g	millet flour
200g	water, hot

Dough

50g	millet leaven
50g	brown rice leaven
100g	millet flour
10g	psyllium husk
5g	salt
130g	water

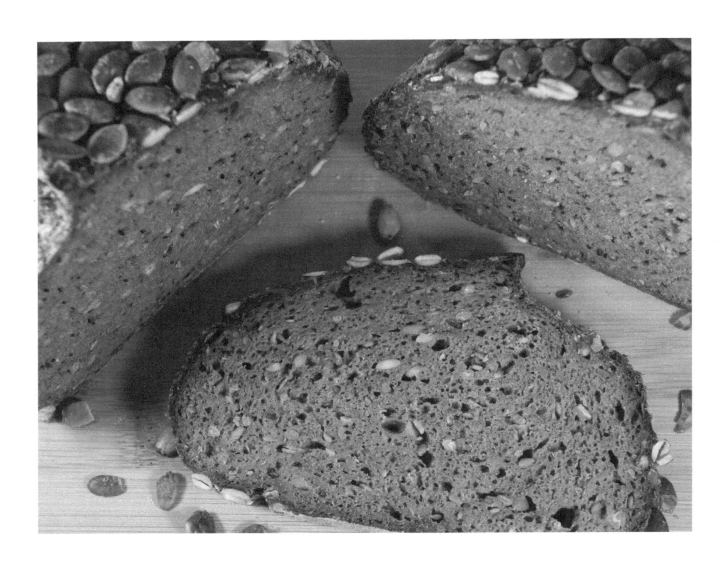

Teff & buckwheat seed loaf

This full flavoured buckwheat and teff boule is ideal for slicing and serving as an open sandwich.

To make this seeded loaf you will need about 100g of seeds. A suggested mix of seeds is provided below. You may have your favourite seeds, or seed mixture, that you would prefer to use. To spice it up, you may consider adding a gram or two of mustard seed or chilli flakes.

Summary

Makes: 1 loaf x 870g

Milling: buckwheat, teff

Hours to prepare: 21 ½ hours

Baking time: 65 minutes

Leaven: buckwheat leaven + teff leaven

Activity	Time	Total
Preparing leaven	0:05	0:05
Fermenting leaven	8:00	8:05
Soaker	(0:30)	8:05
Dough - build 1	0:05	8:10
Dough - build 2	0:05	8:15
Fermenting	8:00	16:15
Shaping	0:05	16:20
Proving	1:00	17:20
Baking	1:10	18:30
Cooling	3:00	21:30

Leaven

This formula uses two separate leavens. Each leaven is developed separately. The two leavens are only brought together in the final dough.

Prepare 50g buckwheat starter and 50g teff starter by mixing each in a separate small bowl.
Cover and allow to ferment for 8 hours.

Soaker

While the leaven is fermenting toast the seeds.
When the seeds have cooled from toasting, place the seeds in a small bowl and add 75g water.
Cover the soaker and to stand until you prepare final dough.

Dough - build 1

Begin mixing the dough one hour before the leaven is ready for use.

In a large mixing bowl mix 200g of buckwheat flour, 100g of teff flour, 12g psyllium husk, and 3g of salt. (Use a whisk to slowly mix all the dry ingredients together, ensure they are thoroughly mixed.)
Mix 300g of water with the dry ingredients.
Cover the unleavened dough and allow to stand for 30 minutes to an hour.

Dough - build 2

When the leaven is ready, mix it, and the remaining 30g of water into the dough - build 1 and mix thoroughly.
Add the soaker to the dough and mix thoroughly.
Cover the dough and allow to ferment for about 8 hours.

Shaping

Turn the dough onto a lightly floured bench (buckwheat flour).
Work the dough gently by spreading and folding four times.
Shape the dough into a rough but hard or boule then place the shaped dough into a suitable banneton.
Use additional seeds to coat the crust at this stage. for sunflower or pepita use 50g, for poppy seed or quinoa 20g should be enough.

Proving

Prove the dough in the banneton for about an hour.
Preheat the oven to 220°C.

Baking

When the oven is ready, dust a peel with a little buckwheat flour, turn the dough out of the banneton, onto the peel.
Score the loaf.
Place the loaf in the oven.
Bake at 220°C with steam for 15 minutes. Remove the metal dish, reduce the temperature to 210°C and continue to bake for a further 50 minutes.

Cooling

Remove the loaf from the oven and place it on a rack to cool.

Soaker

30g	crushed buckwheat seeds
20g	quinoa seeds
20g	flax seeds
10g	sunflower seeds
10g	poppy seeds
5g	pepitas
3g	caraway seeds
2g	fennel seeds
75g	water

Dough - build 1

200g	buckwheat flour
100g	teff flour
12g	psyllium husk
3g	salt
300g	water

Dough - build 2

615g	dough
100g	buckwheat + teff leaven
175g	soaker
30g	water

Leavens

10g	buckwheat starter
20g	water
20g	buckwheat flour
10g	teff starter
20g	water
20g	teff flour

Buckwheat caraway sourdough

When it is milled and baked fresh, buckwheat bread is at its best. This formula uses only buckwheat flour and a buckwheat pre-ferment along with caraway seed to provide a full and delicious buckwheat loaf.

Summary

Makes: 1 loaf x 730g

Milling: buckwheat

Hours to prepare: 19 ½ hours

Baking time: 60 minutes

Leaven: buckwheat leaven

Leaven – pre-ferment

In a medium bowl mix 50g buckwheat starter, 100g water and 100g buckwheat flour.
Cover and set aside the leaven to ferment for around 8 hours.

Dough – build 1

In a large bowl mix 300g buckwheat flour, 12g psyllium husk, 10g caraway seed, and 6g salt.
Mix 300g water with the dry ingredients and combine thoroughly in the bowl.
Cover and allow the unleavened dough to stand until the pre-ferment is ready (approximately 8 hours).

Dough – build 2

When the pre-ferment is ready, mix it into the dough – build 1 and mix thoroughly.

Fermenting

Cover the dough and allow to stand for about 5 hours.

Shaping

Turn the dough onto a very lightly floured bench (buckwheat flour).
Work the dough gently by spreading and folding it twice.
Shape as a rough batard, then place the batard in a banneton.

Proving

Cover the banneton and set aside in a warm, draft free place for about 2 hours.
Preheat the oven to 220° C.

Baking

When the oven ready, dust a peel with a little buckwheat flour.
Turn the dough out of the banneton onto the peel.
Brush or mist the top of the loaf with tepid water, then sprinkle the additional caraway seeds on the top of the loaf.
Allow the loaf to rest for a few minutes to allow any excess water to be absorbed into the crust.
Score the loaf.
Bake with steam at 220° C for 20 minutes. Release the steam (carefully open the oven door, remove the dish if water remains), reduce the temperature to 210° C and continue to bake the loaf for a further 40 minutes.

Cooling

Take the loaf from the oven and place it on a rack to cool for about 4 hours.
This loaf is better rested for 24 hours after baking.

Activity	Time	Total
Prepare leaven	0:05	0:05
Ferment leaven	8:00	8:10
Dough – build 1	(0:05)	8:10
Dough – build 2	0:05	8:15
Fermenting	5:00	13:15
Shaping	0:05	13:20
Proving	1:00	14:20
Baking	1:00	15:20
Cooling	4:00	19:20

Leaven – pre-ferment

50g	buckwheat starter
100g	water
100g	buckwheat flour

Dough

250g	buckwheat leaven
300g	buckwheat flour
10g	caraway seed
12g	psyllium husks
6g	salt
300g	water
2g	caraway seed: additional for dressing the top

Chia & poppy seed bread

This is a sentimental favourite. It is where my love of baking bread began. After a few years of intermittent trial and error I opened the oven to retrieve a loaf that looked and smelled like bread. I don't recall if I stayed in the house or left until it cooled, but the first taste of this bread made an enduring impression: at last I could eat bread without gluten and with comfort and satisfaction. This formula has been modified a little over the years, but for me it remains as a landmark bread.

Summary

Makes: 1 x 775g loaf

Milling: brown rice

Hours to prepare: 6 hours

Baking time: 65 minutes

Leaven: instant dried yeast

Dough

In a large mixing bowl combine the dry ingredients: 260g brown rice flour, 100g tapioca starch, 42g flax meal, 15g psyllium husk, 30g chia seeds, 20g poppy seeds, 20g raw sugar, 5g instant dried yeast, and 6g salt.

Mix 450g tepid water into the dry ingredient.

Mix thoroughly in the bowl.

Mix 15g rice bran oil into the dough. Incorporate the olive oil thoroughly into the dough.

Tip the dough onto a dusted bench and knead by spreading and folding the dough. After about 6 folds roll the dough to a ball and return it to the mixing bowl.

Fermenting

Cover and set dough to ferment for 25 minutes in a warm place, until about double its original volume.

Shaping

Preheat the oven to 210°C.

Turn the dough onto a lightly dusted workbench and knead for a few minutes. Shape dough and place it in oiled bread pan.

For ease of handling halve the dough and place it in the loaf pan in two pieces.

Proving

Cover and set dough to rise for 30 minutes in a warm place.

Baking

Bake, with steam, at 200°C, for 65 minutes.

Cooling

Turn your loaf out of the tin and allow it to cool on a rack for 3 hours.

Activity	Time	Total
Building dough	0:05	0:05
Fermenting	0:25	0:30
Shaping	0:05	0:35
Proving	0:30	1:05
Baking	0:60	2:05
Cooling	3:00	6:05

Dough

260g	brown rice flour
100g	tapioca starch
42g	flax meal
15g	psyllium husks
30g	chia seed
20g	poppy seed
20g	raw sugar
6g	salt
5g	instant dried yeast
10g	oil, olive or rice bran
450g	tepid water

Emperor's batard

Rice is not just rice. There are many different varieties of rice. In this bread Thai black rice (not sticky black rice) is used to create delicious and aromatic bread. Both the aroma and flavour of this bread are reminiscent of Lapsang Souchong tea.

Summary

Makes: 1 x 610g loaf

Milling: black rice, sweet black rice, brown rice

Hours to prepare: 17 ¼ hours

Baking time: 65 minutes

Leaven: brown rice leaven

Leaven

In a medium mixing bowl mix 30g brown rice starter, 150g of water and 150g of sweet black rice flour.
Cover the leaven and set aside for 8 hours to ferment.

Dough – build 1

In a large mixing bowl mix the dry ingredients: 100g black rice flour (not sweet black rice), 100g brown rice flour, 15g psyllium husk, 1g coriander seed, toasted & milled, and 3g salt.
Mix the 200g water into the dry ingredients, combine thoroughly.
Cover the dough and set aside to rest until the leaven is ready.

Dough – build 2

Mix the leaven thoroughly with build 1 dough.
Bassinage: Cover the dough and allow to rest for about 15 minutes.
Mix the remaining 30g of water thoroughly into the dough. Knead dough well for 1 to 2 minutes to ensure the water has all been incorporated into the dough.

Fermenting

Cover the dough and allow to ferment for about 3 hours.

Shaping

Turn the dough onto a lightly dusted bench and gently work the dough into a disc.
The diameter of the disc should be a little less than the length of the proving basket.
Shape the dough as a batard by rolling the disc into a log and tidying up the seam if necessary.
Roll the log in a mixture of white poppyseed and white sesame seed.
Scatter the base of a proving basket lightly with any excess of seed mixture.
Place the dough seam up, in the proving basket.

Proving

Cover the dough and set to rise in a warm place for about 1 hour.
Preheat the oven to 220°C.

Baking

When the oven is ready, dust a peel with a little rice flour, turn the dough out of the proving basket, onto the peel.
Score the loaf deeply.
Place the loaf in the oven.
Bake with steam at 210°C for 65 minutes.

Cooling

Turn the oven off. Open the door briefly to release some heat and steam.
If a baking stone has been used move the loaf to a new position on the baking stone.
Leave the oven door ajar and allow the loaf to remain in a cooling oven for 15 minutes.
Remove the loaf from the oven and place it on a rack to cool for about 4 hours.

This loaf is best if it is allowed to rest 24 hours before cutting.

Activity	Time	Total
Preparing leaven	0:05	0:05
Fermenting leaven	8:00	8:05
Building dough 1	(8:00)	8:05
Building dough 2	0:05	8:10
Fermenting	3:00	11:10
Shaping	0:05	11:15
Proving	1:00	12:15
Baking	0:65	13:20
Cooling	4:00	17:20

Leaven

30g	brown rice starter
150g	sweet black rice flour
150g	water

Dough

330g	black rice leaven
100g	black rice flour
100g	brown rice flour
15g	psyllium husk
3g	salt
230g	water
1g	coriander seed, toasted and milled
5g	white poppyseed
5g	white sesame seed

Extra flour for lightly dusting the bench - either tapioca starch, or a mixture of tapioca starch and fine black rice flour

Leaven

Prepare 350g buckwheat leaven by mixing the ingredients in a medium bowl. Cover and allow the leaven to ferment for 8 hours.

Scald

In a medium jar gradually mix the 150g hot water, 70°C, with the 30g buckwheat flour initially forming a smooth paste, then gradually thin the paste to make a thick gel. Continue to thin the gel until an even, thin liquid is formed.

Cover the scald and allow the scald to malt by keeping it at about 70°C for 8 hours. *See page 42 for information on malting.*

See page 42 for information on malting.

Cool the scald before the next step.

Leaven-Scald

Mix the cooled scald into the bowl of leaven. Cover, and allow to ferment for about 4 hours.

Dough

Mix 150g water and 50g of molasses with the leaven- scald.

In a medium mixing bowl, combine 300g buckwheat flour, 12g psyllium husk, 6g salt, 3g crushed coriander seed, and 2g crushed caraway seed.

Mix the dry ingredients into the leaven-scald mixture and combine thoroughly.

Fermenting

Cover the dough and allow to stand in a warm place for approximately 6 hours.

Shaping

Prepare bread pan by greasing the pan lightly and sprinkling 2g whole coriander seeds in the bread pan.

Turn the dough onto a very lightly floured bench (buckwheat flour).

Work the dough gently by spreading and folding it twice.

Shape as a large roll, then place the roll in a loaf tin.

Homage to Borodinski

Borodinski Bread is a famous Russian rye bread. This homage to Borodinski follows similar methods and techniques to the GOST rules, using buckwheat to create a loaf reminiscent of the famous Russian bread. I have tried to keep both the ingredients and the method as straightforward as possible developing this homage.

When it is milled and baked fresh buckwheat bread is at its best. This formula uses buckwheat flour and a buckwheat starter along with a little molasses, caraway, and coriander seed to provide a delicious buckwheat loaf.

Summary
Makes: 1 x 880g loaf

Milling: buckwheat

Hours to prepare: 26 hours

Baking time: 1hour 25 minutes

Leaven: buckwheat leaven

Proving
Carefully and gently push and smooth the dough into the corners of the loaf tin. A wet hand, or a wet spoon is useful to do this as the dough will be sticky and difficult to handle.

Cover the pan and set the dough aside to prove for about 1 hour.

Moisten, or mist, the top of the dough, with a little water.

Dress the loaf by sprinkling 1g crushed coriander seed on the top of the dough. Continue to prove the dough for another 1 hour while the oven is preheated.

Preheat the oven to 240° C.

The total time allowed for proving the dough is 2 hours: 1 hour initially, then 1 hour after dressing the top with crushed seed.

Baking
Bake, uncovered, at 220°C with steam for 15 minutes.

Cover the tin, reduce the temperature to 200°C and bake for a further 60 minutes. Take the loaf from the oven, carefully remove it from the tin and return the loaf to the oven for a further 10 minutes to dry the crust.

The oven can be switched off for this final stage of baking as there will be enough heat to dry the crust.

Cooling
Remove the loaf from the oven and place it on a rack to cool.

This bread is best if rested for 24 hours before slicing.

Activity	Time	Total
Preparing leaven	0:05	0:05
Fermenting leaven	8:00	8:05
Preparing scald	(0:05)	8:05
Malting scald	(8:00)	8:05
Fermenting leaven-scald	4:00	12:05
Building Dough	0:15	12:10
Fermenting	6:00	18:20
Shaping	0:05	18:25
Proving	2:00	20:25
Baking	1:25	21:50
Cooling	4:00	25:50

Leaven
70 g	buckwheat starter
140 g	water
140 g	buckwheat flour

Scald
30 g	buckwheat flour
150 g	hot water, 70°C

Dough
530 g	leaven-scald
300 g	buckwheat flour
12g	psyllium husks
6g	salt
3g	coriander seed, crushed/milled
2g	caraway seed, milled
150g	water
50g	molasses
2g + 1g	coriander seed, for dressing

Additional buckwheat flour for dusting the workbench

Sorghum multi-seed loaf

For full flavours and nourishment nothing quite beats a slice of multi-seed bread. This formula has its heritage firmly in the line of doughs that were developed from the Chia and Poppy Seed Bread.

Summary

Makes: 1 x 1350g loaf or 2 x 675g loaves

Milling: sorghum

Hours to prepare: 19 ½ hours

Baking time: 70 minutes

Leaven options: millet leaven, or sorghum leaven, or bakers' yeast

1loaf pan: 23cm x10cm x 10cm or

2 loaf pans: 17cm x 10cm x10cm

Leaven

In a large mixing bowl mix 100 g of water with 20g millet starter.

Mix 100 g sorghum flour with the liquid starter.

Cover the leaven and ferment for 8 hours.

Soaker

In a small mixing bowl mix 40g quinoa seed, 30g chia seed, 60g flax seed, 50g sunflower seed, 20g poppy seed, and 2g caraway seed.

Stir in 150g warm water and allow to rest for at least 30 minutes.

Dough

In a large mixing bowl mix the leaven, 300g tepid water, and the soaker.

In a medium mixing bowl mix remaining dry ingredients: 160g sorghum flour, 120g tapioca starch, 40g flax meal, 20g chia meal, 12g psyllium husk, 6g salt. (Do not include the sesame seeds that will form the crust.)

Mix the dry ingredients into the leaven and soaker mixture.

Add the 30g light oil to the dough and mix in well.

Knead the dough gently for a minute. Return the dough to the mixing bowl and cover it.

Set dough to ferment for about 4 hours in a warm place.

Shaping

Preheat the oven to 220°C.

Shape dough into a log by pressing and spreading it gently to form a rectangle, then rolling it so it will fit in the bread pan. Roll the dough log in sesame seeds until seeds cover all the dough.

Place in a lightly oiled bread pan and cover the pan.

Proving

Set dough to rise for 2 hours in a warm place.

Preheat the oven to 210°C

Baking

Bake at 200°C, with steam, for 70 minutes.

Cooling

Turn your loaf out of the bread pan and allow to cool on a rack for 4 hours.

Activity	Time	Total
Preparing leaven	0:05	0:05
Fermenting leaven	8:00	8:05
Soaker	(0:30)	8:05
Building dough	0:05	8:10
Fermenting	4:00	12:10
Shaping	0:05	12:15
Proving	2:00	14:15
Baking	1:10	15:25
Cooling	4:00	19:25

Leaven

20g	millet starter
100g	sorghum flour
100g	water

Soaker

40g	quinoa seed
30g	chia seed
60g	flax seed
50g	sunflower seed
20g	poppy seed
2g	caraway seed
150g	tepid water

Dough

220g	leaven
160g	sorghum flour
120g	tapioca starch
40g	flax meal
20g	chia meal
12g	psyllium husks
352g	soaker
30g	sugar, raw, or honey
6g	salt
30g	light cooking oil
300g	water, tepid

Seeded Crust

30g	sesame seeds

Fruit bread formulas

Red quinoa & prunes

By using a long autolysis, diastatic malt and two leavens, buckwheat and quinoa, and bringing them together for a long, cool ferment a unique loaf of rich and complex flavours is created. For notes on preparing buckwheat diastatic malt flour see page 42.

Leaven

This formula uses two separate leavens. The two leavens are only brought together in the final dough.

Prepare each leaven by mixing the ingredients for each in a separate medium bowl.
Cover the leavens and ferment for 8 hours.

Dough – build 1

In a large mixing bowl mix the dry ingredients: 200g buckwheat flour, 100g red quinoa flour, 5g buckwheat diastatic malt flour, and 12g psyllium husk.
Pour 250g water onto the dry ingredients and mix thoroughly.
Cover and set aside the dough to rest until the leaven is ready.

Dough – build 2

Mix the quinoa and buckwheat leavens into build 1 dough.
Mix in the 2g ground cardamom pods, 2g ground coriander seed, and 4 g fine salt into the dough.
Bassinage: Cover the dough and allow to stand for about 30 minutes.
Add 30 g of filtered water to the dough and work it in thoroughly.
Mix 20g olive oil into the dough.
Spread the dough out, add about 1/4 of the prunes, then fold the dough over.
Repeat this 3 more times until all the prunes have been added into the dough.

Fermenting

Cover the dough and set it aside for about 2 hours to ferment.
Move the dough to a refrigerator to continue fermenting slowly for a further 24 hours.
Remove the dough from the refrigerator and rest at room temperature for an hour.

Shaping

Prepare a proving basket, preferably for a batard.
Place the 60g poppy seed on the workbench.
Turn the dough onto a lightly dusted area of the workbench and shape to a batard or log shape.
Roll the loaf in the poppy seed, ensuring the whole surface of the dough is covered.

Proving

Place the dough in the proving basket.
Cover the dough in the proving basket and set aside to prove for about 1 ½ hours.
While the dough is proving, preheat the oven to 220°C.

Baking

Prepare a peel by dusting it lightly with flour.
Turn the dough from the proving basket onto the peel.
Score the loaf.
Bake, with steam, at 210°C for 65 minutes.

Cooling

Remove the loaf from the oven and place it on a rack to cool for about 3 hours.

Leavens

40g	buckwheat starter
80g	water
80g	buckwheat flour
40g	quinoa starter
80g	water
80g	quinoa flour

Summary

Makes: 1 x 950g loaf

Milling: buckwheat, buckwheat malt, white quinoa, and red quinoa

Hours to prepare: 42 hours

Baking time: 1 hour

Leaven: buckwheat starter + quinoa starter

Activity	Time	Total
Preparing leavens	0:05	0:05
Fermenting leavens	8:00	8:05
Dough - build 1	(0:05)	(0:10)
Dough - build 2	0:35	8:40
Fermenting	27:00	35:40
Shaping	0:05	35:45
Proving	2:00	37:45
Baking	1:15	39:00
Cooling	3:00	42:00

Dough - build 1

200g	buckwheat flour
100g	red quinoa flour
5g	buckwheat diastatic malt flour
12g	psyllium husk
250g	filtered water

Dough - build 2

200g	buckwheat leaven
200g	quinoa leaven
567g	dough build 1
2g	cardamom pods, ground
2g	coriander seed, ground
100g	prunes, pitted and diced
4g	salt, fine
30g	water
20g	olive oil

Additional buckwheat flour for dusting the workbench and the proving basket

Crust

60g	poppy seed

Promise & Fulfilment - real bread without gluten

Spiced millet & currant loaf

For those short winter days and long winter evenings spiced fruits breads are nourishing and comforting. This lightly spiced millet and currant loaf works with the flavours of the flours and spices to provide a tasty and satisfying bread on its own, spread with butter and conserve, or accompanied by cheeses and meats.

Leaven

This formula uses two separate leavens. Each leaven is developed separately. The two leavens are only brought together in the final dough.

Prepare 50g millet leaven and 50g buckwheat leaven.
Set the two leavens aside to ferment overnight, or for about 8 hours at around 20°C.

Dough

Mill 60g chia seeds, 60g flax seeds, 1g cardamom seeds, and 0.5g clove together.
If you are milling the buckwheat groats, these seeds and spices may be mixed through the buckwheat groats and milled together.

In a large mixing bowl combine all the dry ingredients: 240g millet flour, 240g buckwheat flour, 0.5g ginger powder, 5g salt, spiced chia and flax meal, and 100g currants.
Mix milled spices and seeds along with all the dry ingredients gently with a whisk to ensure there are no lumps of milled flax and chia seed.
In a medium bowl, combine the 2 leavens and mix 480g tepid water into the leaven mixture.
Add the leaven mixture to the dry ingredients and combine thoroughly and knead for about 1 minute.

Fermenting

Cover and set dough aside to ferment for approximately 8 hours.

Shaping

Shape the dough into a log and place in a greased loaf tin.

Proving

Set dough to rise for 45 minutes to an hour in a warm place.
Preheat the oven to 210°C.

Baking

Bake at 200°C, with steam, for 60 minutes.

Glaze

The glaze should be prepared a few minutes before the bake completes.

In a small saucepan mix 15g honey and 15g water.
Heat the mixture until boiling, then simmer for up to a minute.
Remove from the heat.

Cooling

When you take the loaf from the oven place it on kitchen paper, on a wire rack. Brush the top of the loaf liberally with the glaze.
Allow the loaf to cool for 3 hours.

Leavens

10g	buckwheat starter
20g	water
20g	buckwheat flour
10g	millet starter
20g	water
20g	millet flour

Summary

Makes: 1 x 1130g loaf

Milling: millet, buckwheat, chia, flax

Hours to prepare: 21 hours

Baking time: 60 minutes

Leaven: millet leaven + buckwheat leaven

Activity	Time	Total
Preparing leavens	0:05	0:05
Fermenting leavens	8:00	8:05
Building dough	0:05	8:10
Fermenting	8:00	16:10
Shaping	0:05	16:15
Proving	0:45	17:00
Baking	0:60	18:00
Cooling	3:00	21:00

Dough

50g	buckwheat leaven
50g	millet leaven
240g	millet flour
240g	buckwheat flour
60g	chia meal
60g	flax meal
100g	currants
1g	cardamom seeds, milled
0.5g	clove, milled
0.5g	powdered ginger
5g	salt
480g	tepid water

Glaze

15g	honey
15g	water

Spiced fruit sourdough

A deliciously spiced fruit loaf to enjoy fresh or toasted.

Use a mixture of dried fruits, or glazed fruits if preferred. If glazed fruits are used be sure not to soak the glazed fruit.

Leaven
This formula uses two separate leavens. The two leavens are only brought together in the final dough.

Prepare 100g quinoa leaven, and 100g buckwheat leaven by mixing the ingredients for each leaven in separate small bowls. Cover and ferment for 8 hours.

Fruit soaker
If glazed fruits are used do not soak the glazed fruits.

If a mix of glazed and dried fruits are used only the dried fruit should be soaked: the soaking water should weigh the same as the dried fruit.

The fruit may need to be cut to ensure all is soaked.

In a small bowl first put 1g cloves, and then 50g of dried fruits.
Pour 50g tepid water over the fruit and leave it to soak.

Dough
In a large mixing bowl combine all the dry ingredients: 150g buckwheat flour, 100g quinoa flour, 100g teff flour, 15g psyllium husks, 1g cinnamon, 1g nutmeg, 2g cardamom, and 4g salt.
In a medium bowl combine the two leavens, 20g honey, and 300g tepid water. Mix the liquid leaven into the dry ingredients.
Add 20g olive oil to the dough and work it in thoroughly.
Remove the cloves from the fruit soaker and add 100g soaked fruits (or 100g glazed fruits) to the dough and mix them into the dough.
Set dough to rise for 4 hours in a warm place.

Shaping
Prepare a lightly greased loaf pan.
Gently knead the dough by spreading and folding the dough three times.
Form a log of dough.
Place the dough log in a loaf pan, seam down.

Proving
Cover the loaf pan and set the dough to rise for 2 hours in a warm place.
Preheat the oven to 210°C.

Baking
Bake with steam, at 200°C, for 60 minutes. While the loaf is baking prepare the glaze: mix 15g honey and 15g water in a small saucepan and stir over a low heat until the honey dissolves and the mixture is almost boiling. Remove from the heat.
Remove from the oven and place on a rack to cool.

Cooling
When you take the loaf from the oven remove it from the loaf pan and brush the top of the loaf liberally with the glaze.
Allow the loaf to cool for at least 3 hours before slicing and serving.

Leavens

20g	buckwheat starter
40g	water
40g	buckwheat flour
20g	quinoa starter
40g	water
40g	quinoa flour

Summary
Makes: 1 loaf x 950g

Milling: quinoa, buckwheat, teff

Hours to prepare: 18 ¼ hours

Baking time: 60 minutes

Leaven: quinoa leaven + buckwheat leaven

Loaf pan: 17cm x 10cm x 10cm

Activity	Time	Total
Preparing leaven	0:05	0:05
Preparing soaker	(0:05)	0:05
Fermenting leaven	8:00	8:05
Building Dough	0:05	8:10
Fermenting	4:00	12:10
Shaping	0:05	12:15
Proving	2:00	14:15
Baking	1:00	15:15
Cooling	3:00	18:15

Fruit Soaker

50g	mixture of dried fruits
1g	cloves (2 cloves)
50g	tepid water

Dough

100g	quinoa leaven
100g	buckwheat leaven
150g	buckwheat flour
100g	quinoa flour
100g	teff flour
15g	psyllium husks
100g	fruit soaker
20g	honey
1g	cinnamon, ground
1g	nutmeg, ground
2g	cardamom, ground
4g	salt
20g	olive oil
300g	tepid water
Buckwheat flour for dusting the bench		

Glaze

15g	honey
15g	water

Buckwheat fruit bread

A rich, spiced fruit loaf that can be prepared in less than 4 hours.

Summary

Makes: 1 x 850g loaf

Milling: buckwheat

Hours to prepare: 3 ¾ hours

Baking time: 50 minutes

Leaven: instant dried yeast

Dough

In a large mixing bowl combine the dry ingredients and fruit: 160g buckwheat flour, 140g brown rice flour, 120g tapioca starch, 15g psyllium husk, 2g cinnamon, 2g pimento, 4g salt, 10g instant dried yeast, 100g dried fruit mixture.

In a medium bowl mix 400g tepid water and 30g raw honey.

Pour the honey water onto the dry ingredients in the large bowl and mix well. Add 10g oil to the dough.

Fermenting

Set dough to rise for 20 minutes in a warm place, until about double its original volume.

Shaping

Lightly dust the work bench and dough. Use either buckwheat flour, or a mix of buckwheat flour and tapioca starch.

Gently knead the dough for a minute.

Shape the dough into a cylinder and place in a loaf tin.
Preheat the oven to 210°C.

Proving

Set dough to rise for 20 minutes in a warm place.

Baking

Bake, with steam, at 200°C for 50 minutes. While the loaf is baking prepare the glaze: mix 15g honey and 15g water in a small saucepan and stir over a low heat until the mixture is almost boiling.
Remove from the heat.

Cooling

When you take the loaf from the oven, remove it from the tin and place on kitchen paper, on a wire rack. Brush the top liberally with the glaze.
Allow the loaf to cool for at least 2 hours before cutting.

Activity	Time	Total
Building dough	0:05	0:05
Fermenting	0:20	0:25
Shaping	0:05	0:30
Proving	0:20	0:50
Baking	0:50	1:40
Cooling	2:00	3:40

Dough

160g	buckwheat flour
140g	brown rice flour
120g	tapioca starch
15g	psyllium husks
30g	raw honey
100g	mixture of dried fruits
10g	instant dried yeast
4g	salt
2g	cinnamon, ground
2g	pimento, ground
10g	light cooking oil
400g	tepid water
Additional buckwheat flour to dust the work bench	

Roll formulas

Sweet rice & quinoa rolls

These light and chewy rolls are delicious on their own, with your favourite fillings, or as an accompaniment with a hearty soup. The flavours of the sweet rice and quinoa combine to produce rich full flavoured roll.

For a more delicately coloured roll use part coloured sweet rice flour and part white sweet rice flour, or part coloured quinoa flour, and part white flour. The rolls pictured on the left are made with 25g black sweet rice and 175g white sweet rice; those on the are made with 50g black sweet rice and 150g white sweet rice.

Summary

Makes: 12 x 60g rolls

Milling: sweet rice, quinoa

Hours to prepare: 20 hours

Baking time: 45 minutes

Leaven options: brown rice leaven, or bakers' yeast

Leaven

Prepare 150g brown rice leaven by mixing the ingredients for each leaven in separate small bowls.
Cover and set aside to ferment for 8 hours.

Dough

In a small mixing bowl mix 200g sweet rice flour, 150g quinoa flour, 12g psyllium husk, 3g salt.
Mix 340g of water into the leaven.
Mix the dry ingredients into the liquid leaven.
Mix 15g rice bran oil into the dough.

Fermenting

Cover the dough and allow to ferment for about 8 hours.

Shaping

Turn the dough onto a lightly floured bench.
Work the dough gently for by spreading and folding 4 times.
Divide the dough into 12 pieces of approximately 70g each.
Shape each piece of dough to a ball or a short finger roll.

Proving

Set the rolls on baking paper lined baking sheet.
Cover and allow to rise for about an hour.
Preheat the oven to 220°C.
Score the rolls.

Baking

Bake at 220°C with steam for 15 minutes. Remove the metal dish, reduce the temperature to 200°C and continue to bake the rolls for a further 30 minutes.

Cooling

When you take the rolls from the oven remove them from the baking sheet and place on a rack to cool for about 2 hours.

Activity	Time	Total
Preparing leaven	0:05	0:05
Fermenting leaven	8:00	8:05
Preparing dough	0:05	8:10
Fermenting	8:00	16:10
Shaping	0:05	16:15
Proving	1:00	17:15
Baking	0:45	18:00
Cooling	2:00	20:00

Leaven

30g	brown rice starter
60g	water
60g	brown rice flour

Dough

150g	brown rice leaven
200g	sweet rice flour (white or coloured)
150g	quinoa flour (white or coloured)
12g	psyllium husk
3g	salt
15g	rice bran oil
340g	water

Toppings

Choose your preferred toppings: seeds or other toppings that will stick to the dough after dipping. Allow up to 5g of topping for 2 bagels.

Buckwheat bagels

This formula uses buckwheat diastatic malt flour and toasted buckwheat flour. See page 42 for information on preparing diastatic malt flour. See page 16 for information on preparing toasted buckwheat flour. Preparation of the flour will take up to 1 day.

Leaven

This formula uses two separate leavens. The two leavens are only brought together in the final dough.

Prepare 50g buckwheat leaven and 50g brown rice leaven by mixing the ingredients for each leaven in separate small bowls.
Cover and set aside to ferment for 8 hours.

Dough

In a large mixing bowl, mix 200g toasted buckwheat flour, 100g brown rice flour, 12g psyllium husk, 5g buckwheat malt flour, and 3g salt.
In a small mixing bowl mix 290g water with the 50g buckwheat leaven and 50g brown rice leaven.
Mix the leaven into the dry ingredients and mix thoroughly.

Fermenting

Cover the dough and allow it to ferment for about 3 hours.

Shaping

On a lightly dusted workbench knead the dough gently by spreading and folding it 4 times.
Divide the dough into 4 pieces of about 184g or 6 pieces each about 122g.
Roll each piece to a 'sausage' with tapered ends, and then overlap and join the ends of each piece to form a bagel.

Proving

Place the bagels on baking sheet lined with baking paper. Cover the bagels and place them in a refrigerator for at least 1 hour, preferably overnight.

Dipping

Preheat the oven to 220° C.
Before preparing the water bath, remove the bagels form the refrigerator and uncover them.
Prepare plates with seeds or your preferred toppings for topping the bagels.
Bring 1000g water to the boil in a large saucepan.
Add 30g molasses to the boiling water.
Place 2 or 3 bagels in the boiling water bath.
Turn each bagel over after 30 seconds to ensure each side is evenly bathed.
Remove each bagel after 60 seconds in the bath using a slotted spatula.
Place bagels on a rack to drain, then place them on the seed plate with the 'top' side down. This ensures the top will be coated with seeds or your preferred topping.
Place the bagels 'top' side down on a baking tray lined with baking paper and cover the bagels.
Set the bagels aside to rest for about 30 minutes while the oven is preheated.

Baking

When the oven is ready, uncover the bagels and place the baking sheet into the middle of the hot oven.
Bake in at 220° C for 20 minutes.
Turn each bagel over, then bake for a further 20 minutes.

Cooling

Take the bagels from the oven and place each one on a rack to cool for about 30 minutes before serving.

Summary

Makes: 4 x 125g or 6 x 80g bagels

Milling: buckwheat, brown rice

Hours to prepare: 15 hours

Baking time: 40 minutes

Leaven: buckwheat leaven + brown rice leaven

Activity	Time	Total
Preparing leaven	0:05	0:05
Fermenting leaven	8:00	8:05
Building dough	0:05	8:10
Fermenting	3:00	11:10
Shaping	0:05	11:15
Proving	1:00	12:15
Dipping	0:05	12:50
Resting	0:30	13:20
Baking	0:40	14:00
Cooling	0:30	14:30

Leavens

10g	buckwheat starter
20g	water
20g	buckwheat flour
10g	brown rice starter
20g	water
20g	brown rice flour

Dough

50g	buckwheat leaven
50g	brown rice leaven
200g	toasted buckwheat flour
100g	brown rice flour
5g	diastatic buckwheat malt flour
12g	psyllium husk
3g	salt
320g	water

Dipping Bath

1000g	water
30g	molasses

Hamburger buns

These are hamburger buns that hold a hamburger together right to the end, taste good and are easy to make.

These hamburger buns can be made with sourdough or with a yeast poolish.

Summary

Makes: 8 x 95g hamburger buns

Milling: brown rice

Hours to prepare: 19 ¾ hours

Baking time: 35 minutes

Leaven options: brown rice leaven, or instant dried yeast

Leaven

Prepare 150g brown rice leaven by mixing the ingredients in a medium bowl.
Cover and set aside to ferment for 8 hours.

Dough

In a large mixing bowl mix all the dry ingredients: 250g brown rice flour, 150g tapioca starch, 30g milled chia seed, 15g psyllium husk, and 6g salt.
Add 440g tepid water and 10g honey to the leaven.
Pour the leaven mixture onto the dry ingredients.
Mix all the ingredients well until the dough comes together.
Add 15g oil to the dough and mix well.

Fermenting

Cover the dough and set it aside to rise for 8 hours in a warm place, until about double its original size.

Shaping

Knead by gently spreading and folding the dough 4 times.
Divide the dough into 8 pieces: about 130g each.
Shape each piece of dough into a flat disk about 10cm in diameter, and place on a lightly floured baking sheet.

Proving

Set the buns to rise for 1 hour in a warm place.
Preheat the oven to 220°C.

Baking

Bake at 200°C, with steam, for 30 minutes, until golden brown.

Cooling

Remove the buns from the oven and place on a rack to cool for 2 hours.

Variation – Leaven

Prepare 150g brown rice poolish by mixing the ingredients.
Cover and set aside to ferment for 8 hours.

1g	instant dried yeast
75g	water
75g	brown rice flour

Activity	Time	Total
Preparing leaven	0:05	0:05
Fermenting leaven	8:00	8:05
Building dough	0:05	8:10
Fermenting	8:00	16:10
Shaping	0:05	16:15
Proving	1:00	17:15
Baking	0:30	17:45
Cooling	2:00	19:45

Leaven

30g	brown rice starter
60g	water
60g	brown rice flour

Dough

150g	brown rice leaven
250g	brown rice flour
150g	tapioca starch
30g	chia seed, milled
15g	psyllium husks
6g	salt
10g	honey
15g	light cooking oil
440g	tepid water
Additional flour to dust the work bench	

Pretzels

Pretzels are a treat. They require a little extra work of dipping them in a bath to partially cook them before baking.

Pretzels are traditionally part cooked in a lye (sodium hydroxide) bath. Lye is caustic and requires special handling. This formula uses bicarbonate of soda instead of lye.

These pretzels may be made with either quinoa or amaranth flour, or a mix of the two, up to the amount listed for the formula.

Of all the gluten free dough I make, this one is the best for shaping. It allows quite intricate shaping, and it holds its shape well through the bath and baking. Remember, it has no gluten, so it can be a little fragile at times, and must be worked gently into its shape.

Dough

In a medium mixing bowl, mix 40g rice malt syrup into 250g tepid water.
In a large mixing bowl mix all the dry ingredients, 150g tapioca starch, 50g arborio rice flour, 100g quinoa flour (or 100g amaranth flour), 12g psyllium husk powder, 5g yeast, 3g salt gently to ensure they are well combined.
Pour the malt syrup mixture onto the dry ingredients and combine thoroughly.
Mix the softened butter into the dough.
Knead until the dough is soft, even and pliable.

Fermenting

Cover the dough and set it aside for 45 minutes to ferment.

Shaping

Before shaping if the dough seems too dry, dip the lump in a little water. Work the lump of dough briefly to incorporate the water.
Lightly dust the workbench and dough with tapioca starch, then gently knead the dough.
Divide the dough into 12 equal portions.
Shape each portion of dough into a 20 cm to 25 cm sausage that is tapered from the middle to the ends.
Place pretzel shaped dough on a baking sheet lined with baking paper, cover shaped dough.

Proving

Preheat the oven to 230°C.
Set dough to rise for about 1 hour in a warm, draft-free place.

Dipping

Bring 1000g water to the boil in the large saucepan or deep frypan.
Add 20g bicarbonate of soda to the water, and maintain a gentle, rolling boil.
A gentle, rolling boil is all that is needed to cook the pretzels. If it is boiling too wildly the pretzel will cook unevenly.

Dip pretzels in the bath for 25 to 30 seconds each. Depending on the size of the bath, you may be able to place more than one at a time.

As you remove each pretzel, allow the excess water to drain, then place on a baking sheet, lined with baking paper.

Baking

The bicarbonate of soda bath partially cooks the pretzels, helps to form and seal the crust, and give the crust its glossy, chestnut brown colour. The more bicarbonate of soda used in the bath, the darker the colour of the crust. So, it is better not to judge if the pretzels are baked by the colour, as colour is not a good measure of whether or not the crumb of the pretzels is adequately baked.

When all pretzels have been dipped, sprinkle pretzels with coarse salt before putting in the oven.
Bake at 220°C for 25 - 30 minutes.

Cooling

Allow the pretzels to cool for 5 minutes before serving while still warm.

Summary

Makes: 12 pretzels

Milling: arborio rice, quinoa / amaranth

Hours to prepare: 2 ¾ hours

Baking time: 30 minutes

Leaven: instant dried yeast

Activity	Time	Total
Building dough	0:05	0:05
Fermenting	0:45	0:50
Shaping	0:05	0:55
Proving	1:00	1:55
Dipping	0:05	2:00
Baking	0:30	2:30
Cooling	0:05	2:35

Dough

50g	arborio rice flour
150g	tapioca starch
100g	quinoa flour (or amaranth flour)
12g	psyllium husk powder
3g	salt
5g	yeast, instant dried
20g	butter, softened
40g	rice malt syrup
250g	tepid water

Dipping

1000g	filtered water
20g	bicarbonate of soda

Finishing

3g	salt, medium to coarse

Bee barm brioche buns

This tasty brioche was inspired by notes about beer barm* in Emmanuel Hadjiandreou's book 'How to Make Sourdough'.

These light and airy, enriched brioche rolls carry the flavour of the bee barm into the brioche rolls.

To prepare the bee barm (honey yeast water) see page 29. To prepare the buckwheat diastatic malt flour see page 42.

* Beer barm is the yeasty residue that remains from brewing beer. This formula prepares a leaven with some of the characteristics of beer barm by using bee barm, or honey yeast water and buckwheat diastatic malt flour.

Leaven – Bee Barm – build 1
In a small mixing bowl or jar mix 15g flour with 5g buckwheat diastatic malt flour. Add 20g bee barm to the malt flour mix. Mix thoroughly.
Allow to ferment for 5 hours.

Leaven – build 2
Mix build 1 leaven with 20g water.
Add 15g flour to the mixture and mix thoroughly.
Allow to ferment for about 4 hours.

Dough
The rice flour may be brown rice or arborio rice, or a mixture of the two. For a softer, lighter bun use 200g arborio rice flour.

In a large mixing bowl mix 75g leaven with milk and eggs.
In a separate bowl mix the dry ingredients.
Add the dry ingredients to the liquid leaven mixture and mix the dough.
Mix the softened butter thoroughly into the dough.

Fermenting
Cover the dough and set aside to ferment for about 6 hours.

Shaping
Divide the dough into six pieces (about 110g each).
Shape each piece into a ball and place on a baking sheet lined with baking paper. Allow plenty of space between the balls of dough.

Proving
Cover the dough and set aside for 1½ hours to prove.
Preheat the oven to 200°C.

Baking
Bake the brioche rolls at 180°C for 45 minutes.

Cooling
When you take the buns from the oven place on a wire rack.
Brush the tops liberally with the glaze.
Allow to cool before serving.

Glaze
The glaze should be prepared a few minutes before the bake completes.

In a small saucepan mix 15g honey and 15g water.
Heat the mixture until boiling, then simmer for up to a minute.
Remove from the heat.

Glaze

15g	honey
15g	water

Summary
Makes: 6 x 85g buns

Milling: buckwheat, brown rice (or arborio rice), buckwheat diastatic malt

Time to prepare: 19 ¾ hours

Baking time: 45 minutes

Leaven: bee barm (honey yeast water)

Activity	Time	Total
Preparing leaven build 1	0:05	0:05
Ferment leaven	5:00	5:05
Preparing leaven build 2	0:05	5:10
Fermenting leaven	5:00	10:10
Building dough	0:05	10:15
Fermenting	6:00	16:15
Shaping	0:10	16:25
Proving	1:30	17:55
Baking	0:45	18:40
Cooling	1:00	19:40

Leaven – build 1

20g	bee barm
5g	buckwheat diastatic malt flour
15g	buckwheat flour

Leaven – build 2

40g	leaven- build 1
20g	water
15g	brown rice flour

Dough

75g	leaven - build 2
200g	rice flour (brown, arborio or a mix)
100g	tapioca starch
15g	psyllium husk powder
3g	salt
200g	tepid milk
50g	softened butter
2	eggs

Buckwheat herb dinner rolls

These quick and tasty dinner rolls use your choice of herbs to complement your menu.

This formula was developed for use by primary school students in the Stephanie Alexander Kitchen Garden Program. This is a nationwide program for pleasurable education that includes planning, planting, growing, harvesting, preparing and sharing food. My aim with these rolls was to help students to prepare tasty, light and enjoyable rolls to share in a class meal.

Summary

Makes: 12 x 45g rolls

Milling: buckwheat

Hours to prepare: 1 ½ hours

Baking time: 25 minutes

Leaven: instant dried yeast

Dough

In a small bowl mix honey & tepid water.
In a large mixing bowl place the 200g buckwheat flour, 100g tapioca starch, 12g psyllium husks, 9g instant dried yeast and 6g salt.
Mix all the dry ingredients gently with a spoon to ensure they are all distributed evenly in the mixture.
Pour the honey water onto the dry ingredients and mix.
When the dough is roughly mixed add the olive oil and herbs.
Mix well in the bowl.

Fermenting

Set dough to rise for 20 minutes in a warm place.

Shaping

Dust the work bench lightly with buckwheat flour.
Turn the dough onto the work bench and lightly roll the dough in the flour so it is easy to handle.
Spread and fold the dough twice.
Divide the dough into 12 lumps of approximately 55g each.
Form each lump into a ball and place on the lined baking sheet allowing about 1.5cm between rolls.
Preheat the oven to 210°C.

Proving

Cover the dough balls and set the dough to rise for about 30 minutes in a warm, draft free place.

Baking

Bake, with steam, at 200°C for 25 minutes.

Cooling

Remove rolls from the oven and place on a rack to cool.

Activity	Time	Total
Building dough	0:05	0:05
Fermenting	0:20	0:25
Shaping	0:05	0:30
Proving	0:30	1:00
Baking	0:25	1:25
Cooling	0:10	1:35

Dough

100g	tapioca flour
200g	buckwheat flour
10g	roughly cut or torn fresh herbs
12g	psyllium husks
9g	instant dried yeast
6g	salt
5g	honey
5g	olive oil
300g	tepid water

Additional tapioca starch for dusting the work bench

Honey pumpkin rolls

These delicious rolls, made with a pumpkin, chia, tapioca, egg and fermented honey can be a welcome relief from the rigours of a limited diet. Most of the time taken is in waiting for the ingredients to ferment. This fermentation provides a lovely complex of flavours. See page 29 for honey yeast water.

Summary

Makes: 6 x 100g rolls

Hours to prepare: 51 hours

Baking time: 35 minutes

Leaven: bee barm (honey yeast water)

Leaven

Mix 10g bee barm, 50g raw honey and 50g water in a lidded glass jar.
Stir and allow to stand, put lid on the jar and give the occasional shake over the next 2 hours until all the honey has dissolved.
When the honey has completely dissolved into the liquid, loosen the lid.
Leave to ferment for about 24 hours after initial mixing.

Pumpkin puree

Bake a piece of pumpkin, about 300g, in an oven at around 180°C for about 35-40 minutes.
Allow the pumpkin to cool, then scoop out the flesh, being careful to get only the flesh, not the skin or the dried baked surface.
Mash the pumpkin flesh to make puree. *Do not add any liquid at this stage.*

Dough

In a large mixing bowl, mix the 200g pumpkin puree, and 100g of bee barm.

The remainder of the bee barm may be returned to the 'starter' jar.

Mix the egg into the puree mixture.
In a medium mixing bowl mix 3g salt, 60g chia meal and 200g tapioca starch.
Mix the dry mix into the puree.
Mix thoroughly ensuring there are no pockets of dry mix. The dough should be smooth and very thick, but sticky.

Fermenting

Cover the dough and allow to ferment for about 20 hours.

Shaping

Line a baking sheet with baking paper.
Dust the bench with a little tapioca starch.
Gently spread and fold the dough about 5 times.
Then shape the dough into a log.
Divide the dough into 6 even lumps, around 100g each.
Roll each lump gently to form a ball. It is important that the dough is rolled.

Proving

Place the rolls, spaced evenly on the lined baking sheet, then cover and allow to rise in a warm place for at least 2 hours.
After about 1 ¼ hours, preheat the oven to 220°C.

Baking

Uncover the rolls and place the baking sheet into the oven.
Bake at 210°C for about 35 minutes.

Cooling

Remove the rolls and place them on a rack to cool for about 2 hours.

Activity	Time	Total
Preparin leaven	2:00	2:00
Fermenting leaven	24:00	26:00
Preparing pumpkin puree	(2:00)	26:00
Building dough	00:05	26:05
Fermenting	20:00	46:05
Shaping	0:05	46:10
Proving	2:00	48:10
Baking	0:35	48:45
Cooling	2:00	50:55

Leaven

10g	bee barm
50g	raw honey
50g	water

Pumpkin Puree

300g	pumpkin, baked

Dough

100g	leaven
200g	pumpkin puree
200g	tapioca starch
60g	chia meal
40g	medium egg
3g	salt

Leaven

In a medium mixing bowl mix 150g yeast water and 100g buckwheat flour.
Cover and set the leaven aside to ferment for about 20 hours at around 26°C.

Dough

In a large mixing bowl, mix dry ingredients: 150g buckwheat flour, 150g tapioca starch, 20g psyllium husks, 30g dark brown sugar, 50g sultanas, 50g candied peel, 1g ground cloves, 1g ground cinnamon, 1g grated nutmeg, 2g ground cardamom, and 5g salt.
Mix 100g eggs (2 eggs), 50g water, and 100g orange juice into the leaven.
Add the leaven mixture to the dry ingredients and mix well in the bowl.
Add 20g olive oil to the dough and combine thoroughly.

Fermenting

Cover the dough and set it aside to rise for 4 hours in a warm place.

Shaping

A little extra buckwheat flour will be required dust the workbench and dough.

Gently knead on a lightly dusted work bench for a few minutes by spreading and folding.

Spiced fruity hot cross buns

Hot Cross Buns, a traditional Good Friday bread, indicate the conflicted relationship the western world has with its Christian heritage. The leaven for this dough is a cultured leaven based on yeast water. It requires a little more planning and work, but you will be greatly rewarded with a bun that has a more complex and rich flavour.

This formula uses yeast water that must be prepared in advance: see page 29.

Summary

Makes: 16 small buns or 9 large buns.

Milling: buckwheat

Hours to prepare: 27 ¼ hours

Baking time: 40 minutes

Leaven: yeast water

Activity	Time	Total
Preparing leaven	0:05	0:05
Fermenting leaven	20:00	20:05
Building dough	0:05	20:10
Fermenting	4:00	24:10
Shaping	0:05	24:15
Proving	2:00	26:15
Applying crosses	0:05	26:20
Baking	0:40	27:00
Cooling	0:15	27:15

To make buns cut the kneaded dough into half, and divide each half into half again, then into quarters. You should now have 16 lumps of dough about the same size, about 60g each.

To make fewer, larger buns divide the dough into 3, then each third into 3. This will give 9 buns of a little over 106g each.

Roll each lump into a ball in the palms of your hands. Place buns on an oiled and dusted baking tray, or into a slice tin.

Proving

Cover the buns and set aside to rise for 2 hours in a warm place.
After 1 ½ hours preheat the oven to 220°C.

Crosses

While buns are proving make the paste for the crosses.

Mix almond meal and tapioca starch together then add water and mix to make a paste.
Spoon the paste into an icing bag with a 3mm (1/8in) nozzle or use a zip-lock sandwich bag with a corner cut to give a similar size opening.
When the buns have risen and are ready to bake, lightly score a cross into the top of each bun, and pipe a cross onto each bun with the paste.

Baking

Bake in a hot oven, 200°C, for 40 minutes.

Glaze

While the buns are baking prepare the glaze. Mix 20g honey and 20g water in a small saucepan and stir over a low heat until the mixture is almost boiling. Remove from the heat.
When you take the buns from the oven brush them liberally with the glaze.

Cooling

Place on kitchen paper on a rack, to cool for about 15 minutes before serving.

Leaven

100g	buckwheat flour
150g	yeast water

Crosses

20g	almond meal
20g	tapioca starch
25g	warm water

Glaze

20g	honey
20g	water

Dough

250g	buckwheat leaven
150g	buckwheat flour
150g	tapioca starch
20g	psyllium husks
30g	dark brown sugar
50g	sultanas
50g	candied peel
1g	cloves, ground
1g	cinnamon, freshly ground
1g	nutmeg, freshly grated
2g	cardamom seed, freshly ground
5g	salt
100g	eggs, 2 medium eggs
100g	orange juice
20g	olive oil
50g	water

Quick milk & currant buns

As a food memory from childhood there is little that compares with soft milk buns. When we bought them, they were finished by filling a slice cut into the top with a little jam and cream. We called them cream buns.

Like many breads, these buns are at their best the day they are made.

Summary

Makes: 9 x 95g buns

Milling: white sorghum, buckwheat

Hours to prepare: 4 ¾ hours

Baking time: 40 minutes

Leaven: instant dried yeast

Dough

Warm 420g whole milk to just below boiling in a small saucepan. Be careful not to boil the milk.
Set the milk aside to cool to around 40°C.

In a large mixing bowl mix the dry ingredients: 170g buckwheat flour, 150g white sorghum flour, 120g tapioca starch, 20g psyllium husk powder, 25g currants, 10g instant yeast, 1g cardamom, and 6g salt. When the milk has cooled to about 40°C, pour the milk and 20g honey onto the dry ingredients and mix the milk in thoroughly. Lightly beat the egg and add it to the dough, mixing in thoroughly.
Add 20g softened butter to the dough and work it in well.

Fermenting

Cover the dough and set it aside to rise for 1 hour in a warm place.

Shaping

Gently knead for a few minutes.
You will require a little extra flour during kneading to dust the work bench. Use either buckwheat flour, or a mix of the buckwheat and tapioca starch if preferred.

Divide the dough into 9 lumps of dough about the same size: around 105g each. Roll each lump into a ball in the palms of your hands. Place buns on greased baking tray, or into a slice tin.

Proving

Preheat the oven to 210°C.
Cover the dough and set it aside to rise for 30 minutes in a warm place.

Baking

Bake, with steam, at 200°C, for 40 minutes.

Glaze

While the buns are baking prepare the glaze. Mix honey and water in a small saucepan and stir over a low heat until the mixture is almost boiling.
Remove from the heat.

Cooling

When you take the buns from the oven, place them on kitchen paper, on a rack to glaze them.
Brush them with the glaze.
Cool for about 2 hours before serving.

Activity	Time	Total
Building Dough	0:05	0:05
Fermenting	1:00	1:05
Shaping	0:05	1:10
Proving	1:00	2:10
Baking	0:40	2:50
Cooling	2:00	4:50

Dough

170g	buckwheat flour
150g	white sorghum flour
120g	tapioca starch
20g	psyllium husk powder
20g	honey
25g	currants
10g	instant yeast
1g	cardamom, milled
6g	salt
20g	butter, softened
1	medium egg
420g	whole milk, tepid

Glaze

15g	honey
15g	water

Variation - Leaven

In a medium mixing bowl, mix 10g rice malt syrup, 75g tepid water, 75g brown rice flour and 4g instant yeast.
Cover and allow to ferment for about 4 hours.

4g	yeast, instant
75g	brown rice flour
75g	tepid water
10g	rice malt syrup

Cinnamon scrolls

Cinnamon Scrolls are one of those comfort foods that are difficult to pass by, but they are even better as a food to share!

To prepare the lievito madre see notes on page 35.

For a simpler variation, instant dried yeast can be used.

Summary

Makes: 8 x 85g scrolls

Milling: arborio rice

Time to prepare: 9 ¾ hours

Baking time: 40 minutes

Leaven options: *lievito madre* or instant dried yeast

Activity	Time	Total
Preparing leaven	0:05	0:05
Fermenting leaven	4:00	4:05
Building dough	0:05	4:10
Fermenting	2:00	6:10
Preparing Cinnamon butter	(0:05)	6:10
Shaping	0:10	6:20
Proving	2:00	8:20
Baking	0:40	9:00
Preparing glaze	(0:05)	9:00
Cooling	0:40	9:40
Glazing	0:05	9:45

Leaven

In a medium bowl mix 50g water, 10g honey or rice malt syrup, and 100g *lievito madre*. Ferment for about 4 hours.

Dough

In a large mixing bowl mix 160g leaven with 200g tepid milk, and 100g eggs (2 large eggs).

In a separate bowl mix the dry ingredients: 200g arborio rice flour, 100g tapioca starch, 15g psyllium husk powder, and 3g salt.

Add the dry ingredients to the liquid leaven mixture and mix the dough thoroughly.

Mix the softened butter thoroughly into the dough.

Fermenting

Cover the dough and set aside to ferment for about 2 hours.

While the dough is fermenting prepare the cinnamon butter.

Cinnamon butter

In a medium mixing bowl combine 50g brown sugar, 10g cinnamon powder, 1g freshly grated nutmeg powder and 100g softened butter.

Shaping

Roll the dough into a rectangle approximately 24cm x 24cm, 1cm thick.

Spread the cinnamon butter evenly across the dough, leaving a 1cm margin along one edge.

Brush the margin with tepid water.

Beginning from the edge opposite the margin, roll the dough into a log.

Cut the log into 8 discs, each 3cm thick.

Arrange the discs on a lined baking sheet, ensuring there is a gap of at least 2cm between the discs, or 3cm between the discs if the scrolls are to be baked without their sides touching.

Proving

Cover the dough and set aside for 2 hours to prove.

Preheat the oven to 200°C.

Baking

Bake the cinnamon scrolls at 180°C for 40 minutes.

When baked, remove the scrolls from the oven and place on a rack to glaze.

Glaze

The glaze should be prepared before the scrolls are removed from the oven and brushed across the scrolls when they are hot from the oven.

In a medium bowl combine 40g softened butter, 30g brown sugar, and 20g hot water.

Brush the glaze over the cooling cinnamon scrolls. It is better to apply a few thinner coats of the glaze rather than one thick coating.

Cooling

Set glazed scrolls aside to cool for at least 15 minutes.

Leaven

100g	*lievito madre*
50g	tepid water
10g	rice malt syrup, or honey

Dough

160g	leaven
200g	arborio rice flour
100g	tapioca starch
15g	psyllium husk powder
3g	salt
200g	milk, tepid
50g	butter, softened
2	large eggs

Cinnamon butter

50g	brown sugar
10g	cinnamon powder
1g	nutmeg, freshly grated
100g	butter, softened

Glaze

40g	butter, salted
30g	brown sugar
20g	hot water

Buckwheat pretzel rolls

Buckwheat pretzel rolls are delicious snack can be eaten as they are for filled with your favourite fillings.

The wholesome flavour of buckwheat is matched with the rich flavours of either quinoa or amaranth. To make them thoroughly enjoyable, top with your preferred topping. I generally sprinkle caraway seed or salt as a topping. You may prefer poppy seed or sesame seed or something else.

This formula can be made using either a natural leaven or bakers' yeast if a sourdough leaven is not available.

Summary

Makes: 12 x 45g rolls

Milling: Brown rice, buckwheat, quinoa

Hours to prepare: 18 ¾ hours

Baking time: 35 minutes

Leaven options: brown rice starter or instant dried yeast

Leaven

In a large mixing bowl mix 100 g of water with 20g brown rice starter.
Mix 100 g buckwheat flour with the liquid starter.
Cover the pre-ferment and leave to ferment for 8 to 10 hours.

Dough

Mix 250g water into the pre-ferment.
Mix the dry ingredients, except seeds for topping, in a separate bowl.
Mix the pre-ferment into the dry ingredients.
Mix 12g olive oil into the dough.
Mix the dough thoroughly.
Cover the dough and allow to stand for about 8 hours.

Shaping

Turn the dough onto a lightly floured bench and work the dough gently by spreading and folding it four times.
Divide the dough into 12 pieces of approximately 65g each.
Shape each piece of dough to a ball, or a short finger roll.
Place the rolls on baking paper, or on a lightly dusted baking sheet.

Proving

Cover the rolls and leave to rise for about one hour.
Towards the end of the hour preheat the oven to 220°C.

Dipping

In a medium or large saucepan boil 1000g of water.
Allow the water to cool briefly so that is not boiling, add 20g of bicarb soda to the water and dissolve it thoroughly.
Return the water to the boil.
Take the rolls, one at a time, and place them in the bath.
Depending on the size of the saucepan you may be to get 4 or 6 in there at one time.

As each roll is removed from the bath allow excess water to drain off.
Place the rolls on a baking sheet that has been lined with baking paper.
Mix the seeds and coarse sea salt, then sprinkle the top of each roll with seed mixture.
Rolls can be topped with poppy, sesame, or caraway seed, or just salt

Score the top of each roll lengthwise.

Baking

When the rolls have all been dipped, sprinkled, and slashed, bake at 200°C for 35 minutes.

Cooling

Remove rolls from the oven and place on a rack to cool for at least 30 minutes.

Variation – Leaven

Prepare the pre-ferment using 1g instant yeast instead of 20g brown rice starter.
Cover the pre-ferment and leave to ferment for 8 to 10 hours.

Activity	Time	Total
Preparing leaven	0:05	0:05
Fermenting leaven	8:00	8:05
Building dough	0:05	8:10
Fermenting	8:00	16:10
Shaping	0:10	16:20
Proving	1:00	17:20
Dipping	0:20	17:40
Baking	0:35	18:15
Cooling	0:30	18:45

Leaven

20g	brown rice starter
100g	buckwheat flour
100g	water

Dough

220g (200g)	leaven
100g	buckwheat flour
100g	tapioca starch
100g	quinoa (or amaranth) flour
12g	psyllium husk
3g	salt
12g	olive oil
250g	water
1g	seed, caraway, poppy, or sesame (for topping)
1g	coarse sea salt (for topping)
Additional buckwheat flour for dusting the work bench	

Crispbread formulas

Brown rice crispbread

It is always good to have crispbread handy. Stored in an airtight container it keeps well. There is little as useful as crispbread in a travel pack – for those times you cannot be certain safety of the food offered, but prefer not to go hungry!

This is a good formula for using accumulated excess starter.

Summary

Makes about: 400g crispbread

Milling: brown rice

Hours to prepare: 16 ½ hours

Baking time: 20 minutes

Leaven options: brown rice leaven or instant dried yeast

Leaven

Prepare 150g brown rice leaven by mixing the ingredients in a medium bowl.
Cover and set aside to ferment for 8 hours.
If 150g accumulated excess starter is used for this dough do not set aside to ferment.

If no sourdough starter is available, the variation provided for yeast can be used.

Dough

Toast the seeds lightly: 10g chia, 10g flax, 5g fennel, 10g poppy and 10g sesame and allow them to cool.
In a medium mixing bowl mix 150g brown rice leaven with 150g tepid water.
In a large mixing bowl mix the 45g toasted seeds, 100g brown rice flour, 50g tapioca starch, 5g psyllium husk, and 4g salt.
Add the leaven mixture to the dry ingredients and mix well.
Add 20g olive oil to the dough and mix well in the bowl.

Fermenting

Set dough to ferment for 4 hours in a warm place.

Shaping

Knead gently by spreading the dough and folding it over 4 times.
Divide the dough into 2 pieces (about 250g each).
Roll each piece of dough to about 2mm to 3mm thick.
Cut cracker shapes and lay out on the lined baking sheet.
The dough may be laid on the lined baking sheet and scored into shapes using a dough cutter or dough scraper instead of using cookie cutters.

Proving

Cover the dough and set it to rise for about 1 hour in a warm place.
Preheat the oven to 220°C

Baking

Dust the dough lightly with salt.
Bake for 20 minutes at 200°C, until golden.

Cooling

Switch the oven off, prop the door open just a little and allow the crispbread to continue baking, then cool in the cooling oven.

Variation – Leaven

In a medium bowl, mix 1g apple cider vinegar, 75g water, 1g instant yeast, then add 75g brown rice flour.

Leaven

75g	brown rice flour	
75g	water	
1g	instant yeast	
1g	apple cider vinegar	

Activity	Time	Total
Preparing leaven	0:05	0:05
Fermenting leaven	8:00	8:05
Building dough	0:05	8:10
Fermenting	4:00	12:10
Shaping	0:05	12:15
Proving	1:00	13:15
Baking	0:20	13:35
Cooling	3:00	16:35

Leaven

30g	brown rice starter
60g	water
60g	brown rice flour

Dough

150g	brown rice leaven
100g	brown rice flour
50g	tapioca starch
10g	chia seed
10g	poppy seed
10g	flax seed
10g	sesame seed
5g	fennel seed
5g	psyllium husks
4g	salt
20g	olive oil
150g	water, tepid

Seeded sourdough rounds

I have always been intrigued by the traditional breads of many shapes and styles. Pictures of crispbread rounds hanging in a kitchen or bakery evoke feelings of mystery and distant cultures. The toasted seeds as well as the fermented flours produce a deep satisfying flavour to accompany preserved fish and meats as well as cheeses and pickles. These crispbread rounds can be stored in the traditional way, and will keep for weeks – unless you eat them first!

The minimum fermentation time is 4 hours. Extending the fermentation will increase the savoury flavour of the crispbread.

Summary

Makes about: 450g of crisp bread.

Milling: quinoa, buckwheat , brown rice

Hours to prepare: 16 hours

Baking time: 30 minutes

Leaven: buckwheat sourdough + quinoa sourdough

Leaven

This formula uses two separate leavens. The two leavens are only brought together in the final dough.

Prepare 50g quinoa starter and 50g buckwheat starter by mixing the ingredeints for each in separate small bowls. Set the two leavens aside to ferment overnight, or for about eight hours at around 20° C.

Dough

Mix all the seeds (caraway, fennel, poppy, flax, and sesame) and toast the seeds gently, stirring occasionally, until they begin to brown, or until they begin to pop. Allow the seeds to cool.
In a small mixing bowl mix 250g water, 50g quinoa leaven and 50g buckwheat leaven.
In a large mixing bowl, mix all dry ingredients: 150g buckwheat flour, 150g brown rice flour, 40g toasted seeds, 5g psyllium husk, and 4g salt.
Pour leaven mixture onto the dry ingredients and mix thoroughly.
Add 30g olive oil to the dough and mix it in thoroughly.
Knead gently for a few minutes.
A little extra flour will be required during kneading to dust the workbench and dough.

Fermenting

Set dough to rise for at least 4 hours in a warm place.

Shaping

Divide the dough into 4 lumps, about 180g each.
Take the lumps of dough one at a time and form a disc about 20mm diameter and 5mm to 8mm thick.
Using a pastry cutter remove the centre of each disc.

Proving

Set dough to rise for 1 hour in a warm place.
Preheat the oven to 220°C.

Baking

Lightly season the discs with salt.
Bake for 45 minutes at 180°C, until mid-brown.

Cooling

Switch the oven off, prop the door open just a little and allow the crispbread to continue baking, then cool in the cooling oven.

Leavens

10g	buckwheat starter
20g	water
20g	buckwheat flour
10g	quinoa starter
20g	water
20g	quinoa flour

Activity	Time	Total
Preparing leaven	0:05	0:05
Fermenting leaven	8:00	8:05
Building dough	0:05	8:10
Fermenting	4:00	12:10
Shaping	0:15	12:25
Proving	1:00	13:25
Baking	0:30	13:55
Cooling	2:00	15:55

Dough

50g	buckwheat leaven
50g	quinoa leaven
150g	buckwheat flour
150g	brown rice flour
10g	poppy seed
10g	flax seed
10g	sesame seed
5g	caraway seed
5g	fennel seed
5g	psyllium husk
4g	salt
30g	olive oil
250g	water

Seeded sourdough thins

A flavoursome crispbread with a lovely, mild, yet complex savoury flavour that comes from the seeds as well as the fermented flours. Ideal for enjoying with soft cheeses or dips.

Summary

Makes about: 350g of crispbread thins

Milling: buckwheat, teff, brown rice

Hours to prepare: 16 hours

Baking time: 25 minutes

Leaven: buckwheat leaven

Leaven

In a medium bowl mix 100g buckwheat starter and 150g water.

Mix 150g buckwheat flour into the mixture.

Cover the bowl or jug and allow the mixture to ferment for around 8 hours

Dough

In a large mixing bowl mix all the seeds (50g hemp, 5g chia, 5g poppy, 5g quinoa, 2g nigella, 5g white sesame, 2g black sesame, and 1g fennel), 50g brown rice flour, 50g teff flour, 5g psyllium husk, and 4g salt.

Mix 400g buckwheat leaven and 50g water into the dry ingredients.

Add 20g olive oil to the dough and mix in well.

Fermenting

Cover the dough and set it to rise for at least 4 hours in a warm place.

The minimum fermentation time for the main dough is 4 hours. Extending the fermentation will increase the savoury flavour of the crispbread. This can be fermented in the refrigerator or up to 24 hours.

Shaping

Knead gently by spreading and folding the dough 4 times.

Divide the dough into 4 pieces (about 170g each).

Roll each piece of dough to about 1mm – 1.5mm thick on a sheet of baking paper. With a dull knife or dough scraper cut cracker shapes.

Lay the dough (still on the baking paper) on the baking sheet.

Proving

Set the dough to rise for about 1 hour in a warm place.

Preheat the oven to 200°C.

Baking

Lightly dress the rolled dough with salt and gently press it into the surface of the dough.

Bake for 25 minutes at 180°C, or until light brown.

If the crackers are allowed to become dark brown, a bitter flavour will develop.

Cooling

Turn off the oven and prop the door open slightly to allow the thins to continue baking and to cool down in the oven.

Activity	Time	Total
Preparing leaven	0:05	0:05
Fermenting leaven	8:00	8:05
Building dough	0:05	8:10
Fermenting	4:00	12:10
Shaping	0:15	12:25
Proving	1:00	13:25
Baking	0:30	13:55
Cooling	2:00	15:55

Dough

400g	leaven
50g	brown rice flour
50g	teff flour
50g	hemp seed, split
5g	chia seed
5g	poppy seed
5g	red or black quinoa seed
5g	sesame seed
2g	nigella seed
1g	fennel seed
2g	black sesame seed
5g	psyllium husk
4g	salt
20g	olive oil
50g	water

Additional buckwheat flour to dust the workbench during kneading and shaping

Additional salt for dressing crispbread

Leaven

100g	buckwheat starter
150g	buckwheat flour
150g	water

Millet grissini

As a small boy one of the treats of visiting grandparents was a meal with soup and bread sticks. Nibbling the grissini and dipping it in the soup was a treat. The memory of soup and bread sticks is one of those fond childhood memories that has not dimmed with age.

Summary

Makes: 16 x 30cm grissini

Milling: millet

Hours to prepare: 18 ¾ hours

Baking time: 35 minutes

Leaven: millet leaven

Leaven

Prepare 50g millet leaven by mixing the ingredients in a small mixing bowl.
Set the leaven aside to ferment overnight, or for about 8 hours at around 20° C.

Dough

In a small bowl mix 260g water with the leaven.
Mix the dry ingredients in a large mixing bowl: 150g millet flour, 150g tapioca starch, and 10g psyllium husk and 3g salt.
Mix the dry ingredients thoroughly.
Add the leaven mixture to the dry ingredients and combine thoroughly.
Mix 30g olive oil to the dough and mix thoroughly.

Fermenting

Cover the dough and allow it to rest for approximately 8 hours.

Shaping

Remove dough from bowl, to a lightly dusted work bench.
Dust the workbench lightly with tapioca starch, or millet flour if it is very fine.
Gently spread and fold the dough.
Roll the dough to a sheet of about 20cm x 30cm and 1cm thick.
Cut the dough to approximately 16 sticks of 1.2 cm x 1cm x 30cm.
Gently twist each piece of dough being careful not to make it longer.
Lay the sticks side by side on a baking sheet lined with baking paper, ensuring the pieces are at least 0.5cm apart.

Proving

Cover the dough sticks and rest for about 1 hour.
Preheat the oven to 220°C.

Baking

Just before baking mist dough sticks with water, or brush with water and sprinkle with seeds (sesame or poppy seeds) and, or flaked salt.
Bake at 200°C for 30 minutes.

Cooling

Switch the oven off, prop the door open just a little and allow the grissini to continue baking, then cool in the cooling oven.

Activity	Time	Total
Preparing leaven	0:05	0:05
Fermenting leaven	8:00	8:05
Building dough	0:05	8:10
Fermenting	8:00	16:10
Shaping	0:05	16:15
Proving	1:00	17:15
Baking	0:30	17:45
Cooling	1:00	18:45

Leaven

10g	millet starter
20g	water
20g	millet flour

Dough

50g	millet leaven
150g	millet flour
150g	tapioca starch
10g	psyllium husk
3g	salt
30g	olive oil
260g	water
5g	seeds for sprinkling
1g	salt for sprinkling

Soda bread formulas

Promise & Fulfilment - real bread without gluten

Millet soda bread

Soda bread is a relatively modern invention. This only leaven used in this bread is bicarbonate of soda.

As it is not fermented the flavour of soda bread is very different from fermented breads prepared with the same ingredients.

Because soda bread contains bicarbonate of soda, a chemical leavening, it does not conform to the UK Campaign for Real Bread. This formula is provided for those who have strict diets that do not allow yeast of any form.

Summary
Makes: 1 x 600g loaf

Milling: millet

Hours to prepare: 3 ¾ hours

Baking time: 35 minutes

Leaven: bicarbonate of soda

Dough
Preheat the oven to 200°C.
Mill chia seeds, flax seeds together into a fine meal.
In a large mixing bowl combine the dry ingredients: 240g millet flour, 60g flax and chia meal, 15g psyllium husk, 4g bicarbonate of soda, and 4g salt. Gently stir the ingredients with a whisk to ensure there are no lumps of seed meal.
Mix 350g water and 10g oil with the dry ingredients.
Mix well in the bowl.
The dough will thicken as you mix it. Keep mixing until you have a kneadable dough.

Shaping
Shape dough and place on a baking sheet. Score the top of loaf before putting in the oven

Baking
Bake, with steam, at 200°C for 35 minutes.

Cooling
Remove from the oven and place on a rack to cool for 3 hours.

Activity	Time	Total
Building dough	0:05	0:05
Shaping	0:05	0:10
Baking	0:35	0:45
Cooling	3:00	3:45

Dough

240g	millet flour
30g	chia meal
30g	flax meal
15g	psyllium husks
4g	bicarbonate of soda
4g	salt
10g	light cooking oil
350g	water

Buckwheat soda bread

The need for a yeast free bread lead to this Buckwheat Soda Bread. The full flavour of buckwheat is complemented with the mild nutty flavours of flax and the mildest of chia in a moist, soft and delicious bread.

Because soda bread contains bicarbonate of soda, a chemical leavening, it does not conform to the UK Campaign for Real Bread. This formula is provided for those who have strict diets that do not allow yeast of any form.

Summary

Makes: 1 x 530g loaf

Milling: buckwheat

Hours to prepare:4 hours

Baking time: 50 minutes

Leaven: bicarbonate of soda

Dough

Preheat the oven to 200ºC.

Mill chia seeds, flax seeds together into a fine meal.

In a large mixing bowl combine the dry ingredients: 240g buckwheat flour, 30g flax and chia meal, 20g psyllium husk, 4g bicarbonate of soda, and 4g salt. Gently stir the ingredients with a whisk to ensure there are no lumps of seed meal.

Mix 300g water and 10g oil with the dry ingredients.

Mix well in the bowl.

The dough will thicken as you mix it. Keep mixing until you have a kneadable dough.

Shaping

Shape dough and place on a baking sheet. Score the top of loaf before putting in the oven

Baking

Bake, with steam, at 200ºC for 50 minutes.

Cooling

Remove from the oven and place on a rack to cool for 3 hours.

Activity	Time	Total
Building dough	0:05	0:05
Shaping	0:05	0:10
Baking	0:50	1:00
Cooling	3:00	4:00

Dough

240g	buckwheat flour
15g	chia meal
15g	flax meal
20g	psyllium husks
4g	bicarbonate of soda
4g	salt
10g	light cooking oil
300g	water

Enriched bread formulas

Savoury poppy seed & honey loaf

A decorative bread enriched with honey and seeds. Even though honey is added to the dough, this is a savoury bread that pairs well with cheeses and charcuterie.

Leaven

Prepare 50g brown rice leaven by mixing the ingredients in a small mixing bowl. Set the leaven aside to ferment overnight, or for about 8 hours at around 20°C.

Dough

Mix 50g brown rice leaven, 50g honey and 300g tepid water in the medium bowl.
In a large bowl combine the dry ingredients: 150g buckwheat flour, 150g brown rice flour, 2g caraway seed, 2g cumin seed, 3g salt and 12g psyllium husk.
Stir the liquid into the flour mix. Combine thoroughly.
Leave the dough to rest for at least 10 minutes.
Turn the dough onto bench flour lightly with some buckwheat flour on the work area.
Knead the dough gently by spreading and folding it three times.

Fermenting

Place the dough in the mixing bowl and cover it and set it aside to ferment for about 8 hours.

Shaping

Turn the dough onto a small pool of oil (about 3 cm) on the work area.
I use olive oil, but you may use your preferred cooking oil.

Oil your hands lightly and gently lift and spread the dough.
Shape the dough into a disk about 1.5cm thick.
Lightly sprinkle the 10g poppy seed, and the 1g nigella seed across the dough, then gently press it into the surface of the dough.
Roll the dough into a log or batard shape.

Proving

Set the dough, seam up, in a banneton or a cloth lined dish to prove the dough.
Cover the dough and leave to prove for about 3 hours.
After 2 to 2 ½ hours preheat the oven to about 220°C.

Baking

Turn the banneton onto a flour dusted baking tray.
Score the top of the loaf.
Bake for about 50 minutes at 210°C.

Cooling

Allow the loaf to cool in the oven for another 10 minutes.
When the loaf is removed from the oven, place it on a rack to cool.

Summary

Makes: 1 x 630g loaf

Milling: buckwheat, brown rice

Hours to prepare: 25 ¼ hours

Baking time: 50 minutes

Leaven: brown rice leaven

Activity	Time	Total
Preparing leaven	0:05	0:05
Fermenting leaven	8:00	8:05
Building dough	0:15	8:20
Fermenting	8:00	16:20
Shaping	0:05	16:25
Proving	3:00	19:25
Baking	0:50	21:15
Cooling	4:00	25:15

Leaven

10g	brown rice starter
20g	water
20g	brown rice flour

Dough

50g	brown rice leaven
150g	buckwheat flour
150g	brown rice flour
12g	psyllium husk
3g	salt
2g	caraway seed
2g	cumin seed
300g	tepid water
50g	honey
10g	poppy seed
1g	nigella seed

Brown rice sandwich loaf

A quick and easy bread is sometimes all we want. This enriched brown rice bread is delicious for sandwiches, or just a slice of bread.

When I developed this bread my family wanted bread that looked and tasted like 'bread'. This bread became our family favourite for everyday bread and school lunches. When my younger daughters were married they each ordered a few loaves of this bread as part of their wedding feasts!

Summary

Makes: 1 x 840g loaf

Milling: brown rice, flax, chia

Hours to prepare: 22 ¼ hours

Baking time: 60 minutes

Leaven: brown rice leaven

Loaf pan: 17cm x 10cm x 10cm

Leaven

In a medium mixing bowl prepare 150g brown rice leaven by mixing the ingredients.
Cover and allow to ferment in a warm, draft free place for 8 hours.

Dough

In a large mixing bowl mix all the dry ingredients: 250g brown rice flour, 100g tapioca starch, 35g flax meal, 15g chia meal, 15g psyllium husks, and 4g salt.
Mix 1 egg, 30g honey, and 300g water into the leaven.
Mix the leaven mixture and 5g light oil into the dry ingredients.
Mix thoroughly.

Fermenting

Cover and set the dough aside to ferment for about 8 hours.

Shaping

Turn the dough onto a lightly dusted bench and gently knead by spreading and folding 4 times.
Shape dough and place in oiled bread pan.
The size of bread pan suitable for this loaf is 17cm x 10cm x 10cm.

Proving

Cover the dough to prove for 2 hours in a warm, draft free place.
Preheat oven to 220°C.

Baking

Bake, with steam, at 210°C for 60 minutes.

Cooling

When you take the loaf from the oven remove it from the pan, and place the loaf on a rack to cool for 3 hours.

Activity	Time	Total
Preparing leaven	0:05	0:05
Fermenting leaven	8:00	8:05
Building dough	0:05	8:10
Fermenting	8:00	16:10
Shaping	0:05	16:15
Proving	2:00	18:15
Baking	1:00	19:15
Cooling	3:00	22:15

Leaven

30g	brown rice starter
60g	water
60g	brown rice flour

Dough

150g	brown rice leaven
250g	brown rice flour
100g	tapioca starch
35g	flax meal
15g	chia meal
15g	psyllium husks
4g	salt
50g	1 large egg
30g	honey
5g	light oil, olive oil, rice bran oil, or sunflower oil
300g	water

Buckwheat & molasses bread

Buckwheat and molasses bread involves combining two strongly flavoured ingredients to produce a rich soft bread. It is somewhat reminiscent of a rye and molasses bread.

Summary

Makes: 1 x 780g loaf

Milling: buckwheat

Hours to prepare: 21 ½ hours

Baking time: 60 minutes

Leaven: buckwheat leaven

Leaven

In a medium mixing bowl weigh 150g water.

Add the 50g buckwheat starter and 150g buckwheat flour to the water and mix thoroughly.

Cover the bowl or jug and allow the mixture to ferment for around 8 hours.

Scald

In small mixing bowl weigh 30g buckwheat flour.

Add 150g boiling water a little at a time, initially create a paste, then gradually dilute the paste until all 150g of boiling water has been added.

Cover the scald and allow it to rest.

Dough

In a large mixing bowl mix all the remaining dry ingredients: 150g buckwheat flour, 12g psyllium husk and 3g salt.

Gently stir the dry ingredients with a whisk to ensure they are well mixed.

Mix the scald and the leaven together in a mixing bowl.

Mix 100g of molasses into the wet mixture.

Mix the wet mixture into the dry ingredients in the large mixing bowl.

Mix well in the bowl.

You should have soft, sticky, but kneadable dough.

Fermenting

Cover the dough and set it to rise for 6 hours in a warm, draft-free place.

Shaping

Gently knead for a few minutes using a dough scraper to spread and fold.

You will require a little extra flour during kneading to dust the kneading board and dough.

Shape dough into a log and place in a well dusted proving basket with the seam up.

Proving

Cover the dough and set it to rise for 2 hours in a warm, draft free place.

Preheat the oven to 220° C

Baking

Dust a peel and turn the dough from the banneton onto the peel.

Score top of loaf before putting in the oven

Bake, with steam, at 200° C for 60 minutes.

Cooling

Remove loaf from the oven and place it on a rack to cool for 4 hours.

Activity	Time	Total
Preparing leaven	0:05	0:05
Preparing scald	0:10	0:15
Fermenting leaven	8:00	8:15
Building dough	0:05	8:20
Fermenting	6:00	14:20
Shaping	0:05	14:25
Proving	2:00	16:25
Baking	1:00	17:25
Cooling	4:00	21:25

Leaven

50g	buckwheat starter
150g	buckwheat flour
150g	water

Scald

30g	buckwheat flour
150g	boiling water

Dough

350g	buckwheat leaven
180g	buckwheat scald
150g	buckwheat flour
100g	molasses
12g	psyllium husks
3g	salt

Leaven

Prepare 50g brown rice leaven by mixing the ingredients in a small bowl.
Cover and set aside the leaven to ferment for at least 4 hours.

Soaker

Do not refrigerate the dough. It will become solid and require warming before building the dough.

It is important that the coconut milk has no additives, particularly gums or thickeners.

Pour 270 g of coconut milk into a large mixing bowl.
Mix 200 g arborio rice flour into the coconut milk.
Cover the soaker and to rest for 4 hours.

Fermenting the leaven and resting the soaker can be done at the same time, overnight. These two activities can continue for up to 10 hours.

Dough

Mix 100g tapioca starch, 12g psyllium husk powder, and 3g salt.
Add the egg and leaven mixture to the soaker in the large bowl.
Mix the remaining dry ingredients into the developing dough.
Mix the dough thoroughly then set aside for about 10 minutes to rest.
Knead the dough gently for about half a minute.

Fermenting

Cover the dough and set it aside in a warm place for about 4 hours to ferment.

Shaping

Remove dough from the bowl to a lightly dusted workbench.
Using a rolling pin, roll the dough to approximately 12 mm thick.
Cut out the doughnut shapes using suitable cutters.
For filled doughnuts use a round cutter about 6 cm to 7 cm in diameter. For doughnuts with holes use a 6 cm to 7 cm cutter for the doughnut, and a 1.5 cm to 2 cm cutter for the hole.

Place shapes on a lightly dusted baking sheet, or a baking sheet lined with baking paper.
Cover the shapes and allow the dough to rise for about 1 hour in a warm place.

Doughnuts

Every now and then a treat is important. My youngest daughter asked me to make her some dairy free doughnuts.

Summary

Makes: 15 doughnuts

Milling: brown rice, arborio rice

Hours to prepare: 10 ½ hours

Cooking time: 20 minutes

Leaven options: brown rice leaven

Cooking

Warning: boiling oil is potentially dangerous. Take care and wear suitable protective clothing for this activity.

Prepare cooking oil in the pan for frying the doughnuts. Oil should be about 2cm deep.

Always use long handled metal tools to place doughnuts in the oil and remove doughnuts from the oil.

Heat the oil to just below boiling point for that oil.

I use rice bran oil and heat it to approximately 185°C.

Place doughnuts, one at a time, into the oil. Allow room between doughnuts for turning and removing doughnuts.
Cook each doughnut for 30 seconds on each side, turning with a spatula.
Place the cooked doughnuts on a cooling rack or on absorbent kitchen paper to allow excess oil to drain.

Dredging/Dusting

Prepare the dredging mixture by mixing 2g ground cinnamon with 50g fine sugar. Place the drained doughnuts, one at a time, into the dredging mixture and spoon or shake the mixture over the doughnut until it has a fine covering of spiced sugar. Set the doughnuts aside to cool.

Filling

Doughnuts should not be filled until they have cooled to room temperature.

For doughnuts filled with jam, fill a piping bag with a suitable nozzle, or a piping syringe with jam. Insert nozzle into the side of the doughnut and fill the doughnut with jam as the nozzle is withdrawn from the dough.
If doughnuts that are to be filled with a cream or similar filling it can be prepared before the doughnuts are cooked.

Cooking oil

The amount used will depend on the size of the pan used for cooking. The oil should be about 2 cm deep. Before heating the oil ensure that the doughnuts can be easily placed in and removed from the oil.

Remember the oil will be boiling hot and dangerous!

Activity	Time	Total
Preparing leaven	0:05	0:05
Preparing soaker	0:05	0:10
Fermenting leaven	4:00	4:10
Building dough	0:15	4:20
Fermenting	4:00	8:20
Shaping	0:15	8:35
Proving	1:00	9:35
Cooking	0:20	9:55
Dredging	0:05	10:00
Cooling	0:30	10:30
Filling	0:05	10:35

Leaven

10g	brown rice starter
20g	water
20g	brown rice flour

Soaker

200 g	arborio rice flour
270 g	coconut milk (additive free)

Dough

50 g	brown rice leaven
470 g	build 1 dough
100 g	tapioca starch
12 g	psyllium husk powder
50 g	water
1	medium egg (45g)
3g	salt

Dredging/Dusting

50 g	fine sugar (caster/confectioners sugar)
2g	ground cinnamon

Filling

100 g	jam or other filling

Fig & walnut loaf

A regional loaf prepared, almost entirely, from ingredients grown in Tasmania.

This loaf has a slightly unusual process as there is only one fermentation. The dough is shaped as soon as it has been built and set to ferment in the proving basket.

Summary

Makes: 1 loaf approximately 950g

Milling: buckwheat, quinoa

Hours to prepare: 23 hours

Baking time: 60 minutes

Leaven: quinoa leaven + buckwheat leaven

Leaven

This loaf uses 2 leavens that are prepared separately and mixed only as the dough is built.

Prepare 30g quinoa leaven and 30g buckwheat leaven by mixing the ingredients for each in separate small bowls. Set the 2 leavens aside to ferment overnight, or for about 8 hours at around 20°C.

Fig & walnut paste

The fig and walnut paste should be prepared before the dough.

Using a food processor or stick mixer blend 50g walnut kernels, 100g dried figs, 50g honey, 50g tepid water and 30g softened butter.
Cover and set aside.

Dough

In a large mixing bowl, mix 30g quinoa leaven, 30g buckwheat leaven, 280g fig & walnut paste and 250g water.
Mix well.
In a medium mixing bowl, mix 100g quinoa flour, 200g buckwheat flour, 12g psyllium husk, and 5g salt.
Mix flour into the leaven and paste mixture.
Mix until well incorporated.
Rest the dough for 30 minutes.
Bassinage: add the remaining 30g water to the dough and mix in thoroughly.

Shaping

Gently knead by spreading the dough and folding it over on itself 3 times.
On a lightly dusted workbench spread the dough to a rectangle about 20 cm x 25 cm. Spread 100g figs (halved), and 50g walnut kernels (halved) on the dough, leaving a 0.5 cm. margin without figs or walnuts along each of the sides.
Beginning with a short edge, roll the dough into a loaf.
Gently press along the seam to seal the dough.
Place the dough seam up in a well dusted proving basket.

Fermenting

Cover the dough and allow to ferment for 10 hours.
About 45 minutes before the end of fermenting, preheat the oven to 220°C

Baking

Bake, with steam, at 200°C for 60 minutes.

Cooling

Remove the loaf from the oven and place on a rack to cool for at least 3 hours.

Leaven

10g	quinoa starter
10g	water
10g	quinoa flour
10g	buckwheat starter
10g	water
10g	buckwheat flour

Activity	Time	Total
Preparing leaven	0:05	0:05
Fermenting leaven	8:00	8:05
Preparing fig & walnut paste	(0:05)	8:05
Building dough	0:40	8:45
Shaping dough	0:05	8:50
Fermenting	10:00	18:50
Baking	0:50	19:40
Cooling	3:00	22:40

Fig & Walnut Paste

50g	walnut kernels, chopped
100g	dried figs, diced
30g	butter, softened
50g	honey
50g	tepid water

Dough

30g	quinoa leaven
30g	buckwheat leaven
100g	quinoa flour
200g	buckwheat flour
280g	fig & walnut paste
12g	psyllium husk
5g	salt
100g	dried figs, halved
50g	walnut kernels, halved
280g	water

Almond paste

In a medium saucepan place 25g water and 65g sugar.

Bring the water and sugar to the boil.

Boil water and sugar on a rolling boil for 1 minute.

Allow sugar liquid to cool.

Add 20g honey and 125g almond meal to the sugar liquid.

Mix honey and almond meal thoroughly with the sugar liquid, then knead the almond paste.

Cover the paste and allow it to rest.

Soaker

In a small bowl mix 75g raisins, 75g mixed peel, 50g slivered almonds and 75g liqueur (brandy, rum, or liqueur).

Cover the soaker and allow to steep.

If you prefer not to use alcohol, you can use 75g of freshly squeezed orange juice or water instead.

Leaven

In a small bowl mix 20g brown rice starter with 100g water.

Add 100g brown rice flour to the water.

Cover and set aside to ferment for about 8 hours.

Dough

In a large mixing bowl mix 140g arborio rice flour, 120g tapioca starch, 45g chia meal & cardamom mixture, 15g psyllium husk powder, and 1g freshly grated nutmeg.

Stir the ingredients gently with a whisk to ensure they are mixed thoroughly and there are no lumps of chia meal.

Add 180g water, 80g eggs, 30g honey to the leaven and mix thoroughly.

Combine the leaven mixture with the dry ingredients in the large mixing bowl. Mix thoroughly.

Cover the dough and rest it for 15 minutes.

Bassinage: Add 30g water to the dough and mix thoroughly.

Stollen

Of all the Christmas breads I find Stollen the most evocative of the festival. A baton of almond paste representing the Son of God wrapped in the bread, the most common of foods, but also a symbol that Son would later use to describe himself: the bread of life.

Summary

Makes: 2 Stollen approx. 680g each

Milling: brown rice, arborio rice

Hours to prepare: 23½ hours

Baking time: 50 minutes

Leaven: brown rice leaven

Add 75g softened butter to the dough and incorporate thoroughly.

Add 275g soaker to the dough and mix it well through the dough.

Fermenting

Cover the dough and set aside in a warm place to rise for about 6 hours.

While the dough is rising prepare two batons of almond paste each about 18 cm long and 2 cm in diameter. Set these aside and cover them to prevent batons from drying out.

Shaping

Remove the dough from the bowl to a dusted bench and divide the dough into two equal portions.

Gently work each piece into a square about 20 cm x 20 cm.

On each square of dough, place a baton parallel to the edge, approximately 5 cm from one edge.

Fold the dough over the almond paste baton and gently seal the baton in the dough.

Place each loaf on a lined baking sheet.

Proving

Cover the loaves and allow to prove for about 2 hours.

Preheat the oven to 210°C.

Baking

Bake at 180°C, with steam, for 50 minutes.

Cooling

Remove the loaves from the oven and allow them to cool for 25 minutes.

Brush the entire crust of each loaf, top and bottom, with softened butter.

Dredge each loaf, top and bottom, with vanilla sugar.

Allow loaves to continue cooling.

When cool store loaves in a sealed container at room temperature.

Serve sliced thinly, approximately 5mm thick.

Almond Paste

125g	almond meal
65g	sugar
20g	honey
25g	water

Soaker

75g	raisins
75g	mixed peel
50g	almond slivers
75g	liquor (brandy or liqueur)

Leaven

20g	brown rice starter
100g	water
100g	brown rice flour

Activity	Time	Total
Preparing almond paste	0:20	0:20
Preparing soaker	0:05	0:25
Preparing leaven	0:05	0:30
Fermenting leaven	8:00	8:30
Building dough	0:30	9:00
Fermenting	6:00	15:00
Shaping	0:10	15:10
Proving	2:00	17:10
Baking	0:50	18:00
Cooling	4:30	22:30

Dough

220g	brown rice leaven
140g	arborio rice flour
120g	tapioca starch
45g	chia meal
15g	psyllium husk powder
80g	2 medium eggs
75g	butter, softened
30g	honey
1	cardamom pod (milled with chia seed)
1g	vanilla paste
1g	nutmeg, freshly grated
200g	water
50g	butter, very soft, not melted
150g	castor sugar, vanilla steeped

Leaven – sponge

The leaven for this formula is lievito madre *that has been bathed in water to reduce the acidity. The* lievito madre *should be prepared in advance: see instructions on page 35.*

In a large mixing bowl mix 200g *lievito madre*, 30g honey, and 280g water.
In a medium bowl mix the dry ingredients: 200g arborio rice flour and 50g proso millet flour.
Mix the dry ingredients into the wet ingredients.
Cover the sponge and set it aside to ferment for about 10 hours.

Soaker

In a tumbler mix 30g sultanas, and 30g candied citrus peel and 10g brandy or orange liqueur.
During dough development stir the brandied fruit from time to time.

Leaven - sponge

200g	*lievito madre*
200g	arborio rice flour
50g	proso millet flour
30g	honey
280g	water

Soaker

30g	sultanas
30g	candied peel
10g	brandy

Panettone

Making panettone is a test of patience and skill that can be richly rewarding. The goal is a light, delicate bread with rich and subtle citrus and fruit flavours.

The use of arborio rice flour allows a more delicate bread to be made. The millet flour helps the dough to maintain its structure.

Panettone is traditionally made with the firm leaven, lievito madre. The washed or bathed lievito madre is used to reduce the acidity of the leaven, and the acidity of the panettone. The lievito madre should be prepared in advance: see notes on page 35.

Summary

Makes 2 x large panettone

(14 cm diameter)

Milling: arborio rice, millet

Hours to prepare: 35 ½ hours

Baking time: 55 minutes

Leaven: lievito madre

Dough

Cut the butter into 10g pieces and set aside to soften.

Mix the dry ingredients: 200g tapioca starch, 50g proso millet flour, 25g psyllium husk powder, 4 g salt, 10g grated lemon rind, and 15g grated orange rind.

Mix all wet ingredients into the sponge: 2g vanilla paste, 30g honey, 25g orange blossom water, 30g calamondin marmalade (or your preferred citrus marmalade), and 100g water.

Mix the sponge mixture into the dry ingredients.

If you are mixing by hand, cover the dough and set it aside to rest for 15 minutes.

If you are using a stand mixer with a dough hook omit the resting period.

One at a time, add and mix into the dough, 5 egg yolks.

Add 120g softened butter, 10g at a time, into the dough, mixing it in before each new addition.

Gently knead the dough until it is smooth and evenly textured.

If you are using a stand mixer with a dough hook, mix the dough on the slowest setting for about 45 minutes.

Towards the end of kneading add the brandied fruit to the dough and mix the fruit evenly through the dough.

Fermenting

Place the dough in a lightly oiled container and seal the container.

Place the dough in the refrigerator for about 10 hours (up to 24 hours).

Remove the dough from the refrigerator. Allow the dough to rest at room temperature (RT) for 1 hour.

Shaping

Divide the dough into 2 equal portions.

Gently knead the dough and shape into a ball.

Place each ball of dough into a paper panettone form.

Proving

Cover each panettone and set aside to rise for about 8 hours in a warm, draft free place.

Preheat the oven to 200°C.

Baking

Bake, with steam, at 180°C for 55 minutes.

Cooling

When baked, prepare the panettone to be turned over, and hung upside down to cool. This can be done by inserting two sturdy skewers through the sides of the baking form, just above the base. The skewers should be long enough to protrude no less than 3cm from the baking form. Support the overturned panettone with the ends of the skewers resting on sturdy supports.

Activity	Time	Total
Preparing sponge	0:15	0:15
Fermenting sponge	10:00	10:15
Building dough	1:00	11:15
Fermenting (cold)	10:00	21:15
Fermenting (RT)	1:00	22:15
Shaping	0:05	22:25
Proving	8:00	30:25
Baking	0:55	31:20
Cooling	4:00	35:20

Dough

745g	sponge
200g	tapioca starch
50g	proso millet flour
25g	psyllium husk powder
4g	salt
10g	grated lemon rind
15g	grated orange rind
2g	vanilla paste
30g	honey
120g	cultured unsalted butter, softened
100g	5 eggs yolks
25g	orange blossom water
30g	calamondin marmalade
100g	water

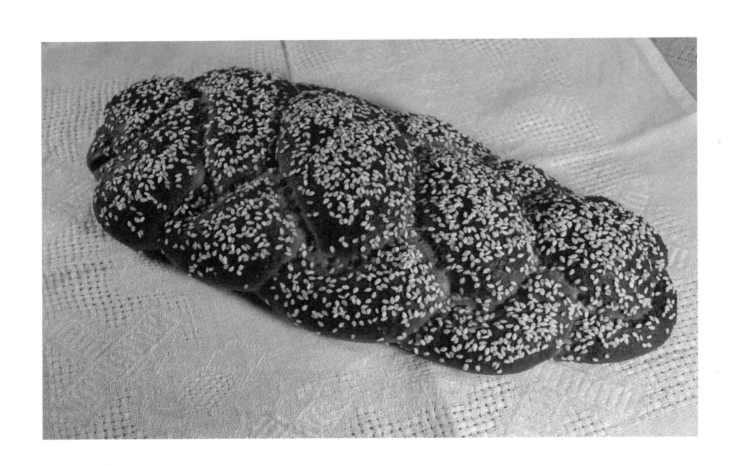

Variation - Leaven:

This formula can use lievito madre *that has been bathed in water to reduce the acidity. The* lievito madre *should be prepared in advance: see information on page 35.*

Mix 100g water and 150g *lievito madre* in a medium bowl.
This leaven is incorporated directly into the dough. No further fermenting of the leaven is required.

Challah

Traditionally used in the Sabbath meal, this enriched bread is dairy free. As a braided bread Challah bears testimony to the baker's skill and patience.

This formula can be challenging. The leaven requires special handling. Either the warm fermented leaven or the alternative use of lievito madre *can be used.*

Summary

Yield: 1 loaf 630g

Milling: buckwheat, brown rice

Hours to prepare: 34 hours

Baking time: 35 minutes

Leaven options: brown rice leaven + buckwheat leaven, or lievito madre

Activity	Time	Total
Preparing leaven	0:05	0:05
Fermenting leaven	10:00	10:05
Building dough	0:15	10:20
Fermenting	20:00	30:20
Shaping	0:10	30:30
Proving	2:00	32:30
Baking	0:35	33:05
Cooling	1:00	34.05

Leaven

10g	brown rice starter
10g	buckwheat starter
100g	buckwheat flour
130g	water

Dough

250g	leaven
100g	buckwheat flour
100g	brown rice flour, fine
100g	tapioca starch
12g	psyllium husk powder
3g	salt
2	large eggs
40g	honey
50g	sunflower oil

Egg wash

1	egg lightly beaten
pinch	salt

Decoration (optional)

5g	sesame seeds or poppy seeds

Leaven

Mix 130g water, 10g brown rice starter, 10g buckwheat starter and 100g buckwheat flour in a medium bowl.
Cover and set the leaven aside to ferment for about 10 hours at around 26° C.

Dough

In a large bowl mix the dry ingredients: 100g buckwheat flour, 100g brown rice flour, 100g tapioca starch, 12g psyllium husk powder, and 3g salt.
Mix the 2 eggs and 40g honey into the 250g leaven.
Combine the leaven mixture with the dry ingredients and work the dough thoroughly until the dough begins to come away from the sides of the bowl.
Gradually add the 50g sunflower oil, 10g at a time, mixing the dough well after each addition. When all the oil has been added continue mixing until the dough looks smooth and silky.

Fermenting

Cover the dough and set it aside to ferment for about 8 hours at room temperature.

Shaping

The dough is delicate, so careful handling is needed during braiding to avoid stretching the strands out of shape, or to unequal lengths.

Prepare a baking sheet lined with baking paper.
Dust the work bench lightly with tapioca starch.
Gently knead the dough by spreading and folding three times.
Divide the dough into 4 equal parts (approximately 190g each).
Roll each part into a smooth ball of dough.
Roll each ball into a strand, 30 cm long, tapered at each end.
Lightly dust the bench with tapioca starch.
Braid the 4 strands of dough.
Carefully move the braided loaf onto the baking sheet.

Proving

Cover the braided loaf and set aside in a warm, draft free place to rise for 2 hours.
Preheat the oven to 200°C.
Prepare the egg wash by gently mixing the egg and pinch of salt together.
Brush the egg wash onto the proved loaf twice. Allow a few minutes between each application.
(If decoration is desired, sprinkle seeds over the braided dough immediately after application of the second wash.)

Baking

Place the loaf in the oven and bake, with steam, at 180°C for 35 minutes.

Cooling

Remove from the oven and place on a rack to cool for at least 1 hour.

Koulouri

Seeded bread rings take many forms: bagels, simit, and koulouri are just a few. These are an interpretation of Greek seeded rings called koulouri. They have honey in the dough and are dipped in pomegranate or grape molasses before coating with sesame seeds.

Summary

Yield: 6 rings of about 12 cm diameter

Milling: brown rice

Hours to prepare: 19 hours

Baking time: 30 minutes

Leaven: brown rice leaven

Leaven

Prepare 50g brown rice leaven by mixing the ingredients in a small bowl.
Cover and set aside to ferment for 8 hours.

Dough

In a large mixing bowl mix the dry ingredients in a large mixing bowl: 150g brown rice flour, 150g tapioca starch, and 15g psyllium husk powder and 3g salt.
Mix the dry ingredients thoroughly.
In a small mixing bowl mix 240g water, 30g leaven, and 20g honey.
Add the leaven and water mixture to the dry ingredients and mix thoroughly.
Add the 30g olive oil to the dough and mix in thoroughly.

Fermenting

Cover the dough and allow it to rest for approximately 8 hours.

Shaping

Remove dough from bowl, to a lightly dusted work bench.
Gently spread and fold the dough.
Divide the dough into 6 equal portions; approximately 110g each.
Shape each piece of dough as finger bun.
Taking the pre-shaped dough one by one, roll each one gently on the bench, drawing it out towards a long sausage shape.
As each piece is rolled out pause, and with a thumb press a line down the centre.
Fold the dough along the line and continue gently rolling the dough.
Continue until the dough is about 45cm long.

Form a ring about 8cm diameter, beginning from the middle, then wind the ends around the ring until a ring of twisted dough is formed.
Repeat with the remaining pieces of dough.

Fermenting

Set the rings aside to rise for about 1 hour.

Dipping & coating

Prepare a mixture of 50g pomegranate or grape molasses and 100g water in a dish large enough to dip the dough rings, one at a time.
Dip each dough ring, then place it on a rack to drain excess liquid.
Coat each ring with toasted sesame seeds.

Proving

Place the dipped and seeded rings on a lined baking sheet.
Cover, and set aside for the final proving: about 45 minutes to 1 hour.
Preheat the oven to 210°C.

Baking

Bake at 200°C, with steam, for 30 minutes.

Cooling

Remove rings from the oven and place on a rack to cool.

Activity	Time	Total
Preparing leaven	0:05	0:05
Fermenting leaven	8:00	8:05
Building dough	0:05	8:10
Fermenting	8:00	16:10
Shaping	0:05	16:15
Fermenting	1:00	17:15
Dipping & coating	0:05	17:20
Proving	1:00	18:20
Baking	0:30	18:50
Cooling	0:15	19:05

Leaven

10g	brown rice starter
20g	water
20g	brown rice flour

Dough

50g	brown rice leaven
150g	brown rice flour
150g	tapioca starch
15g	psyllium husk powder
3g	salt
20g	honey
30g	olive oil
240g	tepid water

Dipping and Coating

50g	pomegranate or grape molasses
100g	water
200g	sesame seeds, toasted

Poppy seed paste

The poppy seed paste should not be prepared until the dough has almost completed its bulk ferment.

Mill poppy seeds, coriander seeds and cardamom seeds in a mill that is suitable for oil seed (otherwise crush the seed using a mortar and pestle).

In a small bowl mix milled poppy seed, coriander seeds, cardamom seeds, softened butter and raw honey to a well combined paste.
Cover and set aside.

Poppy seed paste

100g	poppy seed, crushed
30g	butter, softened
20g	raw honey
2g	coriander seed
1g	cardamom seed (1 pod)

Buckwheat poppy seed scroll

In my younger days I used to look for traditional bakeries that supported local immigrant communities. They always provided the most interesting and flavoursome breads and pastries. This buckwheat and poppy seed scroll was inspired by memories of some of those breads and pastries.

Leaven

This dough uses two separate starters. The starters are kept separate until the dough is built

Prepare 50g brown rice leaven and 50g buckwheat leaven by mixing the ingredients for each in two separate bowls.
Cover the leavens and set aside to ferment for 8 hours.

Dough

In a large mixing bowl, mix the leaven (50g brown rice starter, 50g buckwheat starter), 250g water, 10g olive oil, and 30g raw honey.
In a medium mixing bowl, mix 150g buckwheat flour, 150g brown rice flour, 12g psyllium husk, 3g salt, and 2g caraway seed.
Mix flour into the leaven mixture. Mix until well incorporated.

Fermenting

Cover the dough and allow to ferment for 8 hours.
While the dough is fermenting prepare the poppy seed paste.
Prepare the loaf pan by lightly greasing the pan with butter or your preferred fat.

Shaping

On a lightly dusted bench gently knead the dough by folding and spreading the dough for about 2 minutes.
Gently spread and roll the dough to a rectangle about 20 cm x 25 cm.
Spread the poppy seed mixture across the dough, leaving a 1cm. margin along each side of the dough.
Lightly wet the dough along the margins.
This will help to seal the dough and reduce leakage of the poppy seed mixture from the loaf.

Beginning with one short edge, roll the dough into a loaf.
Gently press along the seam to seal the dough.
Place the dough seam down in a prepared loaf pan.

Proving

Cover the dough and set aside to prove for 2 hours.
Preheat the oven to 220°C.

Baking

Bake, with steam, at 200°C for 50 minutes.
Remove the loaf from the oven, and from the bread pan.

Finishing

Place the loaf on a rack to cool for 15 minutes.
Brush the entire crust with softened butter.

Cooling

Allow the loaf to continue cooling for about 3 hours.

Summary

Makes: 1 x 775g loaf

Milling: brown rice, buckwheat

Hours to prepare: 23 ½ hours

Baking time: 50 minutes

Leaven: brown rice leaven + buckwheat leaven

Activity	Time	Total
Preparing leaven	0:05	0:05
Fermenting leaven	8:00	8:05
Building dough	0:05	8:10
Fermenting	8:00	16:10
Shaping	0:05	16:15
Proving	2:00	18:15
Baking	0:50	19:05
Finishing	0:20	19:35
Cooling	3:00	22:35

Leaven

10g	brown rice starter
20g	water
20g	brown rice flour
10g	buckwheat starter
20g	water
20g	buckwheat flour

Dough

50g	brown rice leaven
50g	buckwheat leaven
150g	buckwheat flour
150g	brown rice flour
12g	psyllium husk
3g	salt
2g	caraway seed
10g	light olive oil
30g	raw honey
260g	water

Finishing

30g	butter, soft but not melted

Viennoiserie formulas

Millet brioche

My first live encounter with brioche was, sadly, years after my doctor put me on a gluten free diet. All I could do was look, smell, prod and regret. The challenge of designing a brioche without gluten was formidable and it was years until I was able to bake a satisfactory brioche. This brioche is rich and almost creamy in texture combining the strength of millet flour with arborio flour to create a dough with a soft creamy texture that is enhanced by both egg and butter.

Summary

Makes: 2 x 330g brioche

Milling: millet, arborio rice

Hours to prepare: 14 ¼ hours

Baking time: 30 minutes

Leaven: millet leaven

Activity	Time	Total
Preparing leaven	0:05	0:05
Fermenting leaven	4:00	4:05
Preparing sponge	0:05	0:10
Fermenting sponge	4:00	8:10
Building dough	0:15	8:25
Fermenting	3:00	11:25
Shaping	0:05	11:15
Proving	1:30	12:45
Baking	0:30	13:15
Cooling	1:00	14:15

Leaven

Prepare 100g millet leaven by mixing the ingredients.

Set the leaven aside to ferment for at least 4 hours.

Sponge

Pour 80g milk into a large mixing bowl along with 100g of leaven and mix it thoroughly

Place 100g millet flour into the milk and leaven mixture and mix it thoroughly.

Cover and set aside for about 4 hours to ferment.

Dough

Cut the 50g stick of butter into small pieces and set them aside to soften.

Lightly beat two eggs and 100g milk in a bowl with 30g honey.

Pour the egg, milk, and honey mixture onto the sponge and combine thoroughly into a smooth batter.

In another mixing bowl mix the remaining dry ingredients: 100g millet flour, 100g arborio rice flour, 15g psyllium husk powder, and 3g salt.

Add the dry ingredients to the Sponge and mix thoroughly.

Cover the dough and set it aside to rest for 5 minutes.

Work the softened butter pieces into the dough.

Knead the dough gently until it becomes smooth with a silky surface.

Fermenting

Cover the dough and allow it to ferment for about 3 hours.

Shaping

Dust the kneading board lightly and gently knead the dough by spreading and folding it twice.

Divide the dough into two equal parts, approximately 340g each.

Divide each part into 4 pieces: three about 80g each, the other about 100g.

Roll each piece into a ball.

Place the 3 x 80g balls into a greased, fluted brioche pan.

Reshape the remaining ball to an egg shape and place the smaller end of the egg, end down, into the middle of the other balls.

Proving

Cover the dough and set aside in a draft free place to rise for 2 hours.

Preheat the oven to 200°C.

Baking

Brush the milk wash onto the proved brioche twice. Allow a few minutes between each application.

Place the brioche in the oven and bake, with steam, at 180°C for 30 minutes.

Cooling

Remove the brioche from the oven. Gently remove each brioche from its tin and allow to cool for 1 hour.

Sponge

100g	millet leaven
100g	millet flour
80g	whole milk

Dough

285g	sponge
100g	arborio rice flour
100g	millet flour
15g	psyllium husk powder
3g	salt
100g	whole milk, tepid
100g	2 large eggs
30g	mild honey (preferably raw)
50g	unsalted cultured butter, softened

Additional flour for dusting the bench during laminating - 1:1 mixture of millet and arborio rice flours

Wash

20g	milk

Leaven

20g	millet starter
40g	millet flour
40g	water

Leaven – *lievito madre*

This formula assumes that lievito madre *is kept and maintained ready for use. See page 35 for notes on* lievito madre.

Allow 8 hours for water bathing. Remove 200g of water bathed *lievito madre* and break it into small pieces.

Dough

The following method is provided for mixing by hand. If using a stand mixer all ingredients for the dough can be mixed in one stage using the dough hook. The butter should only be incorporated when the initial dough has been prepared.

In a large mixing bowl combine 200g *lievito madre*, 260g whole milk, and 40g honey.
In a medium mixing bowl mix 125g fine whole brown rice flour, 75g buckwheat flour, 20g psyllium husk powder, 3g salt. Mix thoroughly.
Add the dry ingredients to the leaven

mixture, mix and combine thoroughly into a smooth dough.
Incorporate the 50g softened butter into the dough.
Knead the dough for about one minute.

Fermenting

Cover the dough and allow to stand for about 2 hours.
Knead the dough gently by spreading and folding 6 times.
Place the dough into neat fitting sealed container or wrap in cling film and refrigerate for at least 4 hours.
The dough may be refrigerated for up to 24 hours.

Laminating the dough

It is important to keep the dough cool during the laminating process. Cultured butter is softer and seems to be better for laminating with this dough.

During lamination dust the dough lightly with fine flour (buckwheat flour or tapioca starch) as required.

Prepare the work bench by chilling, then dust lightly with tapioca starch.
Prepare the butter by placing the 110g butter between the sides of a large piece of folded baking paper. Beat the covered butter with a rolling pin a few times across the whole area of the butter, then using the rolling pin. With the butter folded in the paper, roll the butter into a rough rectangle approx 12cm x 10cm.
Set the butter aside on a cool area of the workbench, or on a chilled plate while the dough is prepared.
On the chilled work bench quickly work the dough into a rough rectangle approx 24cm x 14cm.
Dust the dough very lightly with buckwheat flour.
Place the butter on the dough, in the middle so that the short, 10cm edges,

Wholegrain croissants

When I was a university student, after an overnight journey from Geneva I enjoyed breakfast with other backpackers from the train. That was where I had my first croissant and café au lait. I loved it, and so much else about Paris. About 30 years later I attempted to bake my own croissants. It has been a long journey from that railway café to these gluten free croissants.

In July 2017 I was invited to bake my croissants at Panifica Paris, the boulangerie of Chief Bread Architect François Brault. I am grateful to François for his encouragement, and coaching. The use of lievito madre in these croissants was inspired by Chef Beesham Soogrim, who I had the privilege of meeting at Panifica.

Freshly made sourdough croissants and freshly milled coffee have become a common weekend breakfast in our home.

Summary

Makes: 6 croissants:

Hours to prepare: 27 ½ hours

Milling: Brown rice, buckwheat

Baking time: 25 to 30 minutes

Leaven: lievito madre

are about 1cm from the lower and upper edges of the dough rectangle.

Fold each side of the dough over the butter to enclose the butter within the dough. There should be a small overlap at the middle.

Carefully seal the dough around the butter to ensure butter will not leak out during rolling.

Gently press the dough package with the rolling pin, across the middle, then at each side.

Begin to gently roll the package into a rectangle that is a bit over 2 times as long as it is wide.

1st Fold: Fold the dough in thirds – (letter fold).

Gently press the dough package with the rolling pin, across the middle, then at each side.

Turn the dough so that the direction of rolling will be different to the last rolling. Begin to gently roll the dough into a rectangle that is a bit over 2 times as long as it is wide.

2nd Fold: Fold the dough in half.

Gently press the dough package with the rolling pin, across the middle, then at each side.

Turn the dough so that the direction of rolling will be different to the last rolling. Begin to gently roll the dough into a rectangle that is a bit over 3 times as long as it is wide.

3rd Fold: Fold the dough in half.

Note: The next rolling is the final; the dough is then cut and shaped. The following instructions make 8 smaller croissants. For fewer, larger croissants see the table below for measurements.

Shaping

Gently roll the dough to square approximately 32cm x 32cm.

Trim the square to 30cm x 30cm.

Divide the rectangle into 3 sections 10cm x 30cm.

Divide each section into two long triangles. Beginning at the short edge of each triangle, roll the triangle of laminated dough to a croissant.

Proving

Place croissants on a lined baking sheet. Cover so that nothing is touching the croissants and set aside to prove for around 12 hours in a warm place.

Baking

Preheat the oven to 230°C.

Prepare the egg wash by mixing 1 egg, a pinch of salt, and 15g milk in a tumbler or similar container.

Using a fine pastry brush, brush the croissants with the wash, being careful not to brush the cut edge of the laminations. Cover the wash and set it aside.

Cover the croissants and allow them to prove until oven is ready.

Brush the croissants with the wash for a 2nd time, being careful not to brush the cut edge of the laminations.

Place the croissants, on the lined baking sheet, into the oven. Bake, with steam, at 200°C for 25 to 30 minutes.

Cooling

Remove croissants from the oven and place on a rack to cool.

Activity	Time	Total
Preparing leaven	8:00	8:00
Building dough	0:20	8:20
Fermenting dough	6:00	14:20
Laminating dough	0:20	14:40
Shaping croissants	0:05	14:45
Proving	12:00	26:45
Baking	0:30	27:15
Cooling	0:15	27:30

Dough

200g	lievito madre
125g	fine brown rice flour
75g	buckwheat flour
20g	psyllium husk powder
3g	salt
50g	butter, softened
260g	whole milk
40g	honey, raw
110g	unsalted cultured butter for laminating

Additional buckwheat flour to dust the dough before placing the butter package for laminating

Additional buckwheat flour or tapioca starch to dust the bench during laminating.

Wash

1 pinch	fine salt
1	egg
15g	milk

Leaven

This formula uses a water kefir leaven. This leaven can become very active late in the fermentation. Use a medium bowl (at least 1 litre capacity) to prepare the buckwheat kefir leaven.

Mix 150g kefir water and 100g buckwheat flour in a medium bowl.
Cover and set the leaven aside to ferment for about 20 hours at around 26° C.

Dough

The dough is tempered by freezing, then defrosting slowly in the refrigerator.

Hydration of the dough may vary depending on your buckwheat flour. If the dough seems too dry, add more liquid 10g at a time, mixing it in thoroughly until pliable dough is formed. If the dough seems too moist, add more buckwheat flour 10g at a time, mixing it in thoroughly until pliable, but not overly soft, dough is formed.

Successful lamination of the dough with butter depends on both the dough and the butter deforming at approximately the same rate. If the dough is too firm it is likely to crack and allow butter to escape. If the dough is too soft the butter may break rather than flow during lamination. If you need to depart from the amount of liquid or flour stated in this formula be careful to record the changes, as well as other information, like room temperature, so you have clear records for making adjustments in future.

In a large mixing bowl mix the dry ingredients: 200g buckwheat flour, 15g psyllium husk powder, 3g salt.
Pour 160g milk into the bowl containing the leaven.
Add the 10g molasses to the leaven and milk, then mix the milk and molasses into the leaven.
Pour the leaven mixture onto the dry ingredients mix and combine thoroughly into a smooth dough.

Knead the dough for about one minute.

Tempering the dough

Place the dough into neat fitting sealed container, or wrap in cling-film and freeze for about 8 hours.
Remove the dough from the freezer and defrost in the refrigerator (approximately 6 hours).

Laminating the dough

It is important to keep the dough as cold as possible during the laminating process.
Prepare the work bench by chilling.
Prepare a packet for the butter by folding a sheet of baking paper to make a 10cm x 15cm pouch.
Prepare the butter by placing the 125g butter inside the pouch of folded baking paper. Beat the covered butter with a rolling pin a few times across the whole area of the butter, then using the rolling

Buckwheat croissants

After developing a good croissant with rice, I set out to explore other possibilities. Buckwheat is grown organically at a farm not far from my home. I enjoy making bread with the lovely flour I mill from this pseudo-grain, so why not try a croissant with the same flour?

My early trials caught the attention of a friendly baker in Greece who encouraged me to continue the work to develop a 100% buckwheat croissant. This formula is the result of that work.

Summary

Makes: 6 croissants:

Milling: buckwheat to a fine flour

Hours to prepare: 44 hours

Baking time: 30 minutes

Leaven: water kefir leaven

Activity	Time	Total
Preparing leaven	0:05	0:05
Fermenting leaven	20:00	20:05
Building dough	0:15	20:20
Tempering dough	14:00	34:50
Laminating	0:20	35:10
Shaping	0:05	35:15
Proving	8:00	43:15
Baking	0:30	43:45
Cooling	0:15	44:00

pin, roll the butter into a rough square approx 10cm x 15cm.

Set the butter aside on a cool area of the workbench, or on a chilled plate while the dough is prepared.

Dust the workbench lightly with fine buckwheat flour.

On the chilled work bench quickly work the dough into a rough rectangle approx 15cm x 22cm.

Lightly dust the surface of the dough with fine buckwheat flour.

Unwrap the butter package and place it in the middle of the dough sheet so that the long sides of the butter are at right angles to the long sides of the dough sheet.

Fold the dough from the sides across the butter. The two edges of the dough sheet should meet in the centre of the butter. Fold the top and bottom of the dough sheet over the butter, and gently seal all the edges so the butter is fully enclosed in the dough sheet.

Roll the dough package gently, dusting as needed, and repairing any breaks in the dough to ensure the butter does not escape, until the dough sheet is approximately 30cm x 20cm.

1st Fold: lightly mark the dough into three rectangles 20cm x 10cm. Fold the rectangle on one side across the middle rectangle, then fold the remaining rectangle from the other side across to complete a folded dough package that is approximately 20cm x 10cm.

Turn the dough so that the direction of rolling will be different to the last rolling. Begin to gently roll the dough into a rectangle that is approximately 30cm x 20cm.

2nd Fold: Fold the dough package in half so that it is approximately 15cm x 20cm. Turn the dough so that the direction of rolling will be different to the last rolling.

Begin to gently roll the dough into a rectangle that is approximately 30cm x 20cm.

3rd Fold: Fold the dough package in half so that it is approximately 15cm x 20cm. This is the final fold.

Shaping

Roll the pastry out to a rectangle of approximately 30cm x 30 cm. The dough sheet is now ready for cutting and shaping the croissants.

Cut the sheet into 3 rectangles, each 30cm x 10cm.

Cut each rectangle on the diagonal to produce 2 long, right angled triangles. Before rolling the triangles gently stretch the right angled corner to produce a triangle where the long sides are approximately the same length.

Gently roll the croissants, one at a time, rolling from the short side to the vertex of the two longer sides.

Proving

Cover the croissants and set aside in a warm place, 20°C to 24°C for at least 8 hours.

Baking

Preheat the oven to 220°C.

Prepare the egg wash by whisking 1 egg, a pinch of salt and 20g milk in a small bowl. Wash the croissants twice, allowing a few minutes between washes.

Bake at 180°C for 30 minutes.

Cooling

Remove from the oven and cool before serving.

Leaven

100g	buckwheat flour
150g	kefir water

Dough

250g	buckwheat kefir leaven
200g	buckwheat flour
15g	psyllium husk powder
3g	salt
160g	whole milk
10g	olive oil
10g	molasses
125g	unsalted cultured butter

Additional buckwheat flour for dusting during laminating.

Wash

1	egg
pinch	salt
20g	milk

Olive oil brioche

This formula was inspired by Tartine's Olive Oil Brioche, set as a 'Bread of the Month' challenge for members of a Facebook sourdough group in 2016. The result is a delicious brioche with the richness of egg, the complex flavours provided by long fermentation.

Summary

Makes: 1 x 740g loaf

Milling: brown rice, white sorghum

Hours to prepare: 24 hours

Baking time: 35 minutes

Leaven: brown rice leaven + bee barm

Leaven

The leaven consists of two pre-ferments, one made with bee barm the other with brown rice starter.

Pre-ferment 1

This pre-ferment is made with bee barm, see page 29 for more information. Another yeast water can be substituted. If no yeast water is available, use 0.5g of instant yeast or 1g fresh yeast, along with 40g water and 40g sorghum flour to prepare the pre-ferment.

In a small mixing bowl mix 40g bee barm and 40g sorghum flour into the yeast water.
Cover and set aside for 8 hours.

Pre-ferment 2

Mix 30g brown rice starter and 45g water in a small mixing bowl.
Mix 45g brown rice flour into the starter mixture.
Cover and set aside for 8 hours.

Dough

In a medium bowl mix the dry ingredients: 150g sorghum flour, 100g brown rice flour, 50g tapioca starch, 10g psyllium husk powder, and 3g salt.
In a large bowl mix the 2 eggs, 50g water, 80g pre-ferment 1, 120g pre-ferment 2, 30g honey, and 10g orange blossom water.
Mix the dry ingredients into the leaven mixture.
Mix the dough thoroughly until the dough easily comes away from the sides of the bowl.
Gradually add the 60g olive oil 10g at a time, when all the oil has been added continue mixing until the dough looks smooth and silky.

Fermenting

Cover the dough and set it aside to ferment form about 2 hours at room temperature.
Gently knead the dough by spreading and folding 3 times.
Return the dough to the bowl, or an oiled, lidded container. Cover and place in the refrigerator overnight.

Shaping

Prepare bread pan by brushing with olive oil.
Turn the dough onto a lightly oiled work bench and shape into a cylinder.
Place the dough, seam down, into the bread pan.

Proving

Cover the dough and set aside in a draft free place to rise for 2 hours.
Preheat the oven to 200°C.

Baking

Prepare the egg wash by gently mixing the egg and salt together.
Brush the egg wash onto the brioche twice. Allow a few minutes between each application.
Place the loaves in the oven and bake at 180°C for 35 minutes.

Cooling

Remove the brioche from the pan and place on a rack to cool for 3 hours.

Egg wash

1	egg, lightly beaten
pinch	salt, fine

Activity	Time	Total
Preparing leaven	0:05	0:05
Fermenting leaven	8:00	8:05
Building dough	0:15	8:20
Fermenting	10:00	18:20
Shaping	0:05	18:25
Proving	2:00	20:25
Baking	0:35	21:00
Cooling	3:00	24:00

Pre-ferment 1

40g	sorghum flour
40g	bee barm

Pre-ferment 2

30g	brown rice starter
45g	brown rice flour
45g	water

Dough

80g	pre-ferment 1
120g	pre-ferment 2
150g	sorghum flour
100g	brown rice flour
50g	tapioca starch
10g	psyllium husk powder
3g	salt
100g	2 large eggs
50g	water
30g	honey
10g	orange blossom water
60g	extra virgin olive oil

Leaven – pre-ferment

Prepare 200g of *lievito madre*.
See page 35 for information about lievito madre.

In a large mixing bowl mix 150g whole milk, 200g *lievito madre* and 100g arborio rice flour.
Cover and set aside to ferment for about 10 hours.

Dough

Lightly beat 3 medium eggs in a bowl with 40g honey.
Pour the egg and honey mixture onto the preferment and mix well.
In medium mixing bowl combine the remaining dry ingredients (100g tapioca starch, 50g buckwheat flour, 25g psyllium husk powder, and 6g salt).
Add the dry ingredients to the pre-ferment and mix thoroughly.
Cut the 60g stick of softened butter into small pieces and work it into the dough.
Knead the dough for about one minute.

Fermenting

Cover the dough and allow it to rest on the bench for about 1 hour.
Place the dough in the refrigerator to chill the dough for a least 10 hours.
Dough can be chilled longer, but it is best laminate this dough within 24 hours.

Laminating the dough

It is important to keep the dough cold during the laminating process.

Prepare the work bench by chilling, then dust lightly with tapioca starch.
Prepare the butter by placing the 120g butter between the leaves of a large piece of baking paper folded in half. Beat the covered butter with a rolling pin a few times across the whole area of the butter, then using the rolling pin, roll the butter into a rough square approximately 19cm x 19cm.
Set the butter aside on a cool area of the workbench while the dough is prepared.
On the chilled work bench quickly work the dough into a rectangle approximately 20cm x 40cm.

Brioche feuliettée

Laminating is a skill that takes dedication and practice. It is not easily gained. This final brioche combines the learning from many other breads, providing a light, feathery crumb that melts in the mouth as it should.

Lightly dust the dough with buckwheat flour.

Place the square of butter in the middle of the dough rectangle.

Fold each side of the dough over the butter to enclose the butter within the dough.

Gently press the dough package with the rolling pin, across the middle, then at each side.

Begin to gently roll the package into a rectangle that is a bit over 2 times as long as it is wide.

1st Fold. Fold the dough in half.

Gently press the dough package with the rolling pin, across the middle, then at each side.

Turn the dough so that the direction of rolling will be different to the last rolling.

Begin to gently roll the dough into a rectangle that is a bit over 2 times as long as it is wide.

2nd Fold. Fold the dough in half.

Gently press the dough package with the rolling pin, across the middle, then at each side.

Turn the dough so that the direction of rolling will be different to the last rolling.

Begin to gently roll the dough into a rectangle that is a bit over 2 times as long as it is wide.

3rd Fold. Fold the dough in half.

Roll the dough to a rectangle 50cm x 20cm.

Shaping
Fold the two long edges to the middle of the rectangle so that it is 50cm x 10 cm.

Fold the dough into a concertina 5cm high x 10cm wide.

Place the concertina block gently into the loaf pan.

Proving
Cover and set aside to prove for about 9 hours.

Preheat the oven to 200°C.

Using a pastry brush, brush the top of the loaf with whole milk.

Be careful not to allow milk to run off the top crust down the sides of the loaf pan as this will cause the crust to stick to the pan during baking.

Baking
A baking tray can be placed beneath the perforated loaf pan to catch any escaping butter.

Bake, with steam, at 180°C for 40 minutes.

Cooling
Remove from the oven and allow to stand for a few minutes before removing the loaf from the pan.

Place on a rack to cool for 3 hours.

Summary
Makes: 1 loaf about 600g

Milling: arborio rice, buckwheat

Hours to prepare: 34 ¼ hours

Baking time: 40 minutes

Leaven: *lievito madre*

Perforated loaf pan, 22cm x 11.5cm x 7cm

Activity	Time	Total
Preparing leaven	0:05	0:05
Fermenting leaven	10:00	10:05
Building dough	0:05	10:10
Fermenting	11:00	21:10
Laminating	0:20	21:30
Shaping	0:05	21:35
Proving	8:00	29:35
Baking	0:40	31:15
Cooling	3:00	34:15

Leaven - preferement

200g	*lievito madre*	
100g	arborio rice flour	
150g	whole milk	

Dough

450g	pre-ferment	
100g	tapioca starch	
50g	buckwheat flour	
25g	psyllium husk powder	
6g	salt	
120g	egg, 3 medium eggs	
40g	mild honey (preferably raw)	
60g	butter, unsalted cultured, softened	
120g	butter, unsalted cultured, for laminating	

Additional tapioca starch for dusting the bench during laminating.

Wash

20g	milk	

Resources

Key Ingredient Chart:

	page number	amaranth	chestnut	buckwheat	millet	quinoa	rice	sorghum	teff	tapioca starch	psyllium husk	chia	flax	diastatic malt
Basic bread														
Millet & Buckwheat Cottage Loaf	51			180g	225g						10g	50g	30g	
Quinoa Sourdough	53					260g				150g	12g	50g		
Buckwheat, Quinoa & Teff	55			230g		100g			50g		12g			
Millet Sandwich Loaf	57				255g					100g	12g			
Kindred Flax Loaf	59			400g		15g							70g	
Buckwheat & Chestnut	61		75g	250g		25g					12g			
Buckwheat Pumpernickel	63			305g#										5g
Quinoa, Sweet Rice, & Buckwheat Loaf	65			165g		75g	75g swr				12g			4g
Baguettes														
Amaranth Baguettes	69	100g					25g br			200g	12g			
Buckwheat & Chestnut Baguettes	71		75g	100g			25g br			150g	12g			
Rice Baguettes	73						175g br			150g	15g			
Millet Baguettes	75				175g					150g	12g			
Flat Breads														
Millet Focaccia	79				205g					100g	12g			
Olive Fougasse	81				225g		100g ar				12g			
Pita	83				200g					100g	15g			
Pizza Dough	85			50g^	200g^	50g^	150g br			150g	15g p			
Rice & Chia Wraps	87						100g br / 50g swr				5g	20g		
Seeded Breads														
Sunshine Loaf	91				175g		225g br				10g			
Teff & Buckwheat Seeded Loaf	93			255g#					125g		12g			
Buckwheat Caraway Sourdough	95			425g							12g			
Chia & Poppy Seed Bread	97						260g br			100g	15g	30g		
Emperor's Batard	99						115g br / 150g swb / 100g blr				15g			
Homage to Borodinski	101			505g							12g			
Sorghum Multi-seed Loaf	103				10g	40g#		260g		120g	12g	50g#	100g#	

Key Ingredient Chart:

Category	Recipe	page number	amaranth	chestnut	buckwheat	millet	quinoa	rice	sorghum	teff	tapioca starch	psyllium husk	chia	flax	diastatic malt
Fruit Breads	Red Quinoa & Prune Loaf	107			300g		100g, 100g rq					12g			5g
Fruit Breads	Spiced Millet & Currant Loaf	109			265g	265g							60g	60g	
Fruit Breads	Spiced Fruit Sourdough	111			200g		150g			100g		15g		60g	
Fruit Breads	Buckwheat Fruit Bread	113			160g			140g br			120g	15g			
Fruit Breads	Sweet Rice & Quinoa Rolls	117					150g	75g br / 200g swr				12g			
	Buckwheat Bagels	119			25g, 200g tb			125g br				12g			5g
Rolls	Hamburger Buns	121						325g br			150g	15g	30g		
Rolls	Pretzels	123					100g	50g ar			150g	12g			
Rolls	Bee Barm Brioche Rolls	125			15g			215g br			100g	15g			5g
Rolls	Buckwheat Herb Dinner Rolls	127			200g						100g	12g			
Rolls	Honey Pumpkin Rolls	129									200g	12g	60g		
Rolls	Spiced & Fruity Hot Cross Buns	131			250g						150g	20g			
Rolls	Quick Milk & Currant Buns	133			170g				150g		120g	20g			
Rolls	Cinnamon Scrolls	135			50g^	50g^	50g^	200g ar			100g	15g			
Rolls	Buckwheat Pretzel Rolls	137			200g		100g	10g br			100g	12g			
Crispbread	Brown Rice Crispbread	141						175g br			50g				
Crispbread	Seeded Sourdough Rounds	143			175g	25g		150g br				5g	10g	10g	
Crispbread	Seeded Sourdough Thins	145			200g		5g rq#	50g br		50g		5g	10g	10g	
Crispbread	Millet Grissini	147				175g					150g	12g			

ar = arborio rice; br = brown rice, blr = black rice; bw = buckwheat; rq = red quinoa; swb = sweet black rice, swr = sweet rice; p = psyllium husk powder; tb = toasted buckwheat

Unless otherwise indicated the quantity of flour includes flour used in the leaven. ^ indicates 50g of the flour is in the leaven. # indicates seed is included

Key Ingredient Chart:

Flours +

Category	Recipe	page number	amaranth	chestnut	buckwheat	millet	quinoa	rice	sorghum	teff	tapioca starch	psyllium husk	chia	flax	diastatic malt
Soda	Millet Soda Bread	151				240g						15g	30g	30g	
Soda	Buckwheat Soda Bread	153			240g							20g	15g	15g	
Enriched Bread	Savoury Poppy Seed & Honey Loaf	157			150g			175g br				12g			
Enriched Bread	Brown Rice Sandwich Loaf	159						325g br			100g	15g	15g	35g	
Enriched Bread	Buckwheat & Molasses	161			355g							12g			
Enriched Bread	Doughnuts	163						25g br			100g	12g p			
Enriched Bread	Fig & Walnut Loaf	165			215g		115g	200g ar				12g			
Enriched Bread	Stollen	167						110g br			120g	15g p			
Enriched Bread	Panettone	169			50g^	150g^	50g^	140g ar			200g	25g p			
Enriched Bread	Challah	171			205g			105g br			100g	12g p			
Enriched Bread	Koulouri	173						175g br			150g	15g p			
Enriched Bread	Buckwheat Poppy Seed Scroll	175			165g			165g br				12g			
Viennoiserie	Millet Brioche	179				250g		100g ar				15g p			
Viennoiserie	Wholegrain Croissants	181			125g^	50g^	50g^	125g br				20g p			
Viennoiserie	Buckwheat Croissants	183			350g							15g p			
Viennoiserie	Olive Oil Brioche	185				50g^	50g^	150g br	190g		50g	10g p			
Viennoiserie	Brioche Feuilettée	187			100g^	50g^	50g^	100g ar			100g	25g p			

ar = arborio rice; br = brown rice; blr = black rice; bw = buckwheat; rq = red quinoa; swb = sweet black rice; swr = sweet rice; p = psyllium husk powder; tb = toasted buckwheat

Unless otherwise indicated the quantity of flour includes flour used in the leaven.   ^ indicates 50g of the flour is in the *lievito madre*. # indicates seed in included

Leavens

Category	Item	bee barm	brown rice	buckwheat	instant yeast	lievito madre	millet	quinoa	teff	water kefir	yeasat water
Basic bread	Millet & Buckwheat Cottage Loaf						✓				
Basic bread	Quinoa Sourdough							✓			
Basic bread	Buckwheat, Quinoa & Teff			✓							
Basic bread	Millet Sandwich Loaf						✓				
Basic bread	Kindred Flax Loaf							✓			
Basic bread	Buckwheat & Chestnut				+			+			
Basic bread	Buckwheat Pumpernickel			✓							
Basic bread	Quinoa, Sweet Rice, & Buckwheat Loaf	✓		✓							
Baguettes	Amaranth Baguettes	✓									
Baguettes	Buckwheat & Chestnut Baguettes	+		+							
Baguettes	Rice Baguettes	✓									
Flat Breads	Millet Baguettes						✓				
Flat Breads	Millet Focaccia						✓				
Flat Breads	Olive Fougasse						✓				
Flat Breads	Pita						✓				
Flat Breads	Pizza Dough					✓					
Flat Breads	Rice & Chia Wraps	✓									
Flat Breads	Sunshine Loaf	+					+				
Seeded Breads	Teff & Buckwheat Seeded Loaf			+					+		
Seeded Breads	Buckwheat Caraway Sourdough			✓							
Seeded Breads	Chia & Poppy Seed Bread					✓					
Seeded Breads	Emperor's Batard	✓									
Seeded Breads	Homage to Borodinski			✓							
Seeded Breads	Sorghum Multi-seed Loaf						✓				
Fruit Breads	Red Quinoa & Prune Loaf				+			+			
Fruit Breads	Spiced Millet & Currant Loaf				+		+				
Fruit Breads	Spiced Fruit Sourdough				+			+			
Fruit Breads	Buckwheat Fruit Bread					✓					

Key Ingredient Chart:

Leavens

Category	Item	bee barm	brown rice	buckwheat	instant yeast	lievito madre	millet	quinoa	teff	water kefir	yeasat water
Rolls	Sweet Rice & Quinoa Rolls		✓								
Rolls	Buckwheat Bagels		+	+							
Rolls	Hamburger Buns		✓								
Rolls	Pretzels					✓					
Rolls	Bee Barm Brioche Rolls	✓									
Rolls	Buckwheat Herb Dinner Rolls					✓					
Rolls	Honey Pumpkin Rolls	✓									
Rolls	Spiced & Fruity Hot Cross Buns										✓
Rolls	Quick Milk & Currant Buns					✓					
Rolls	Cinnamon Scrolls					✓					
Rolls	Buckwheat Pretzel Rolls		✓								
Crispbread	Brown Rice Crispbread		✓								
Crispbread	Seeded Sourdough Rounds			+					+		
Crispbread	Seeded Sourdough Thins			✓							
Crispbread	Millet Grissini								✓		
Soda	Millet **Soda** Bread										
Soda	Buckwheat **Soda** Bread										
Enriched Bread	Savoury Poppy Seed & Honey Loaf		✓								
Enriched Bread	Brown Rice Sandwich Loaf		✓								
Enriched Bread	Buckwheat & Molasses				✓						
Enriched Bread	Doughnuts		✓								
Enriched Bread	Fig & Walnut Loaf				+				+		
Enriched Bread	Stollen		✓								
Enriched Bread	Panettone					✓					
Enriched Bread	Challah		+	+							
Enriched Bread	Koulouri		✓								
Enriched Bread	Buckwheat Poppy Seed Scroll		+	+							
Viennoiserie	Millet Brioche							✓			
Viennoiserie	Wholegrain Croissants					✓					
Viennoiserie	Buckwheat Croissants									✓	
Viennoiserie	Olive Oil Brioche		+	+							
Viennoiserie	Brioche Feuilettée					✓					

* Please check your ingredients: molasses sometimes contain sulphites; dried fruits often contain sulphites.

✓ The formula is free from this ingredient.

Free From Advice: All are free from oats, soy, peanuts, celery, fish, crustaceans, molluscs, corn, lupins and mustard.

	The listed formula are free from	Page	egg	dairy	psyllium husk	flax	chia	nuts	maize/corn	sesame	sulphites
Basic bread	Millet & Buckwheat Cottage Loaf	51	✓	✓			✓	✓	✓	✓	✓
Basic bread	Quinoa Sourdough	53	✓	✓		✓	✓	✓	✓	✓	✓
Basic bread	Buckwheat, Quinoa & Teff	55	✓	✓		✓	✓	✓	✓	✓	✓
Basic bread	Millet Sandwich Loaf	57	✓	✓		✓	✓	✓	✓	✓	✓
Basic bread	Kindred Flax Loaf	59	✓	✓	✓	✓	✓	✓	✓	✓	✓
Basic bread	Buckwheat & Chestnut	61	✓	✓		✓	✓		✓	✓	✓
Basic bread	Buckwheat Pumpernickel	63	✓	✓	✓	✓	✓	✓	✓	✓	✓
Basic bread	Quinoa, Sweet Rice, & Buckwheat Loaf	65	✓	✓		✓	✓	✓	✓	✓	✓
Baguettes	Amaranth Baguettes	69	✓	✓		✓	✓	✓	✓	✓	✓
Baguettes	Buckwheat & Chestnut Baguettes	71	✓	✓		✓	✓	✓	✓	✓	✓
Baguettes	Rice Baguettes	73	✓	✓		✓	✓	✓	✓	✓	✓
Baguettes	Millet Baguettes	75	✓	✓		✓	✓	✓	✓	✓	✓
Flat Breads	Millet Focaccia	79	✓	✓		✓	✓	✓	✓	✓	✓
Flat Breads	Olive Fougasse	81	✓	✓		✓	✓	✓	✓	✓	✓
Flat Breads	Pita	83	✓	✓		✓	✓	✓	✓	✓	✓
Flat Breads	Pizza Dough	85	✓	✓		✓	✓	✓	✓	✓	✓
Flat Breads	Rice & Chia Wraps	87	✓	✓		✓		✓	✓	✓	✓
Seeded Breads	Sunshine Loaf	91	✓	✓		✓	✓	✓	✓	✓	✓
Seeded Breads	Teff & Buckwheat Seeded Loaf	93	✓	✓		✓	✓	✓	✓	✓	✓
Seeded Breads	Buckwheat Caraway Sourdough	95	✓	✓		✓	✓	✓	✓	✓	✓
Seeded Breads	Chia & Poppy Seed Bread	97	✓	✓	✓	✓		✓	✓	✓	✓
Seeded Breads	Emperor's Batard	99	✓	✓		✓	✓	✓	✓	✓	✓
Seeded Breads	Homage to Borodinski	101	✓	✓		✓	✓	✓	✓	✓	*
Fruit Breads	Sorghum Multi-seed Loaf	103	✓	✓		✓	✓	✓	✓	✓	✓
Fruit Breads	Red Quinoa & Prune Loaf	107	✓	✓		✓	✓	✓	✓	✓	*
Fruit Breads	Spiced Millet & Currant Loaf	109	✓	✓	✓	✓	✓	✓	✓	✓	*
Fruit Breads	Spiced Fruit Sourdough	111	✓	✓		✓	✓	✓	✓	✓	*
Fruit Breads	Buckwheat Fruit Bread	113	✓	✓		✓	✓	✓	✓	✓	*
Rolls	Sweet Rice & Quinoa Rolls	117	✓	✓		✓	✓	✓	✓	✓	✓
Rolls	Buckwheat Bagels	119	✓	✓		✓	✓	✓	✓	✓	*

Free From Advice:
All are free from oats, soy, peanuts, celery, fish, crustaceans, molluscs, corn, lupins and mustard.

✓ The formula is free from this ingredient.
* Please check your ingredients: molasses sometimes contain sulphites; dried fruits often contain sulphites.

The listed formula are free from	Page	egg	dairy	psyllium husk	flax	chia	nuts	maize/corn	sesame	sulphites
Rolls										
Hamburger Buns	121	✓	✓		✓	✓	✓	✓	✓	✓
Pretzels	123	✓	✓		✓	✓	✓	✓	✓	✓
Bee Barm Brioche Rolls	125	✓	✓		✓	✓	✓	✓	✓	✓
Buckwheat Herb Dinner Rolls	127	✓	✓		✓	✓	✓	✓	✓	✓
Honey Pumpkin Rolls	129	✓	✓		✓	✓	✓	✓	✓	✓
Spiced & Fruity Hot Cross Buns	131		✓		✓	✓	✓	✓	✓	✓
Quick Milk & Currant Buns	133				✓	✓	✓	✓	✓	*
Cinnamon Scrolls	135						✓	✓	✓	✓
Buckwheat Pretzel Rolls	137	✓	✓		✓	✓	✓	✓	✓	✓
Crispbread										
Brown Rice Crispbread	141	✓	✓		✓	✓	✓	✓		✓
Seeded Sourdough Rounds	143	✓	✓		✓	✓	✓	✓		✓
Seeded Sourdough Thins	145	✓	✓		✓		✓	✓	✓	✓
Millet Grissini	147	✓	✓		✓	✓	✓	✓	✓	✓
Soda										
Millet Soda Bread	151	✓	✓		✓	✓	✓	✓		✓
Buckwheat Soda Bread	153	✓	✓		✓	✓	✓	✓	✓	✓
Enriched Bread										
Savoury Poppy Seed & Honey Loaf	157	✓	✓		✓	✓	✓	✓	✓	*
Brown Rice Sandwich Loaf	159	✓	✓			✓	✓	✓	✓	✓
Buckwheat & Molasses	161	✓	✓		✓	✓	✓	✓	✓	*
Doughnuts	163	✓	✓		✓	✓	✓	✓	✓	✓
Fig & Walnut Loaf	165	✓			✓	✓		✓	✓	✓
Stollen	167				✓	✓	✓	✓	✓	✓
Panettone	169				✓	✓	✓	✓		✓
Challah	171	✓	✓		✓	✓	✓	✓	✓	✓
Koulouri	173	✓	✓		✓	✓	✓	✓		*
Buckwheat Poppy Seed Scroll	175	✓			✓	✓	✓	✓	✓	✓
Viennoiserie										
Millet Brioche	179				✓	✓	✓	✓	✓	✓
Wholegrain Croissants	181				✓	✓	✓	✓	✓	✓
Buckwheat Croissants	183				✓	✓	✓	✓	✓	✓
Olive Oil Brioche	185		✓		✓	✓	✓	✓	✓	✓
Brioche Feuilettée	187				✓	✓	✓	✓	✓	✓

Uses for sourdough starter

If I have excess sourdough starter, how can I use it? That question is asked from time to time. The obvious answer is: 'Bake more bread!' That isn't always helpful. As gluten-free flours are expensive it is good to develop a discipline of keeping a small 'mother' and not developing an excess of starter, but sometimes we find ourselves with more than we need, and we simply don't want to throw out our little community of microbes. So, what do we do?

First, don't discard, accumulate! If you keep more than one starter it is easy to accumulate starter if you keep all your starters *en pointe*. Keeping an accumulator jar in the refrigerator is a simple way of collecting enough starter to prepare for making other items like crispbread, pancakes, waffles and crumpets. The photograph below shows my accumulator jar with about 300g of a mixture of brown rice starter, millet starter, brown teff starter, ivory teff starter, and quinoa starter.

Using formulas from this book

My favourite use of accumulated starter is crispbread. I often accumulate a jar of starter to make crispbread - it is very useful as a travelling food. The formula for Brown Rice Crispbread on page 141 can be prepared with 150 grams of accumulated starter.

The formula for Rice and Chia Wraps on page 87 can be prepared with 100 grams of accumulated starter.

A few simple uses for starter

Starter, especially mature starter with well developed exopolysaccharides, makes a good batter for frying. So, spice it up, mix in some vegetables and make pakora. Or, thin it just a little and use the starter as a tempura batter.

Three formulas for accumulated starter

The following formulas for pancakes, waffles, and crumpets have been designed to use excess or accumulated starter well.

Sourdough pancakes

Makes: 10 x 12cm pancakes

Hours to prepare: 2 hours

Cooking time: 10 minutes

Leaven: sourdough starter

300g	ripe sourdough starter
100g	buckwheat flour
150g	water or milk
2	eggs
30g	sunflower oil or olive oil
30g	honey
6g	salt

Method

In a large mixing bowl mix 300g ripe sourdough starter, 150g water (or milk), 2 eggs, 30g oil, 30g honey, and 6g salt.

Cover the batter and set aside in a warm place for at least 1 hour to ferment.

Heat a large, heavy skillet to a medium/high heat. Grease with butter to provide a non-sticking surface to the skillet.

Stir the fermented batter to ensure the ingredients have not separated during fermentation.

Spoon or pour batter onto the skillet.

When the top of the batter has set, turn the pancake over to lightly cook the top before removing from the skillet to a cooling rack, or serving plate.

Sourdough waffles

Makes: 10 waffles

Hours to prepare: 2 hours

Cooking time: 15 minutes

Leaven: sourdough starter

500g	ripe sourdough starter
3	eggs
50g	sunflower oil
30g	honey
6g	salt

Method

In a large mixing bowl mix 500g ripe sourdough starter, 3 eggs, 50g sunflower oil, 30g honey, and 6g salt.

Cover the batter and set aside in a warm place for at least 1 hour to ferment.

Prepare a waffle iron by heating and greasing if needed.

Stir the fermented batter to ensure the ingredients have not separated during fermentation.

Spoon or pour batter into the waffle iron.

Close the waffle iron and cook for a few minutes. If the waffle iron is electrical there should be a thermostat-controlled light to indicate when the waffles are cooked. If the waffle iron is a heated over a flame or coals, turn the iron over every 30 seconds and check the waffles after 3 minutes.

Extra waffles can be cooled and frozen for a lazy day, or for a quick treat for visitors.

Sourdough crumpets

Makes: 6 x 8cm crumpets

Hours to prepare: 2 hours

Cooking time: 30 minutes

Leaven: washed *lievito madre*

200g	*lievito madre*
100g	tapioca starch
6g	salt
2	eggs
30g	olive oil
150g	tepid water

Method

In a large mixing bowl mix 200g water bathed *lievito madre* with 2 eggs, 30g olive oil, 150g tepid water, 100g tapioca starch, and 6g salt.

Cover the batter and set aside in a warm place for at least 1 hour to ferment.

Prepare 4 x 8cm diameter egg rings by greasing with butter.

Heat a large, heavy skillet to medium heat. Grease lightly with butter to provide a non-sticking surface to the skillet.

Place the egg rings in the heated pan.

Stir the fermented batter to ensure the ingredients have not separated during fermentation.

Spoon or pour batter into the rings to between a depth of between 1cm and 1.5cm.

Cook slowly covering the skillet to retain warmth.

When the top of the batter has set, either remove the crumpets from the skillet and place on a cooling rack to remove the rings or, turn the crumpets over to lightly cook the top before removing from the skillet to a cooling rack. Remove the rings.

Check the rings and re-grease if needed before cooking another batch.

Please don't panic ...

Troubleshooting issues with sourdough starter:

What could possibly go wrong with sourdough starter?

Here are a few things:

Concern	Possible cause & explanation	Action
No obvious signs of fermentation.	This is a common concern with 100% buckwheat starters. It is most likely fine. Buckwheat can be a very unspectacular starter. If it is fermenting there will be tiny bubbles, lots of tiny bubbles. Those tiny bubbles indicate that the starter is active. You may see bigger bubbles at some stage, but you may not. Buckwheat starter has low yeast levels compared with the lactic acid bacteria. The combined activity of the lactic acid bacteria and the yeast will provide adequate leavening for the dough. Often a 100% buckwheat starter will provide very good oven spring.	Don't panic. It is normal for 100% buckwheat.
It smells horrid!	From time to time starters will grow kahm yeast. It usually only settles water or on a watery film on the top layer of the starter. This happens especially when the starter is wet. I find I get it on buckwheat starter more than any other starter.	Recovery is fairly straightforward: you need at least three sterile (scalded) spoons and freshly scalded jar. With the 1st spoon scrape away the top 1cm from the starter. With the 2nd spoon take away another layer. The stuff you have removed is waste. As you remove these layers be careful not to mix into the lower starter. Next, use a 3rd sterile spoon to dig out about 30g of starter. This goes into the fresh, sterile jar. Now refresh the starter in the new sterile jar with 30g water, 30g flour. Cover the jar with a solid lid. Refresh again by discard (i.e. 30g starter, 30g water, 30g flour) in another fresh sterile jar within 24 hours.
It has something growing on it.	This is more serious and more difficult to provide general advice about recovering the starter. If it is a yeast what you are seeing is the fruit of the mycelium that is already established in your starter. It may be safe, it may not be safe. It is possible that the 'infection' has come from flour. If you use pre-milled flour check the flour for 'off' aromas. If you mill your own flour, check your seed for problems. (You may need to clean your mill thoroughly if you have been milling contaminated seed. Check with the mill manufacturer for recommended cleaning procedures.)	Unless you are able to identify the source of the growth and confirm that it is safe, the best action is to dispose of the starter and prepare a new culture. When you begin a new culture ensure that all your implements and containers are clean and sterile.

Troubleshooting issues with sourdough starter:

What could possibly go wrong with sourdough starter?

Here are a few things:

Concern	Possible cause & explanation	Action
It is changing colour.	There are a few reasons for the starter to change colour: 1. Fungal/mould/yeast growth 2. Bacterial growth 3. Oxidation of the top layer 4. Drying of the top layer Items #1 & #2 indicate that the starter has not been maintained well. There is likely to be a changed aroma in the container. Be careful not to inhale directly from the container as you may inhale spores if it is #1. See the discussion about growths on the starter. Items #3 & #4 indicate the humidity in the starter container has not been adequate, and that the starter needs to be refreshed. If #3 is the problem there will be a thin layer of darker starter on the top.	For colour changes due to #1 & #2: dispose of the starter and prepare a new culture. For colour changes due to #3 & #4: using a sterile spoon remove the top 1cm of starter. Refresh the starter and cover with a covering that will retain the humidity in the air above the starter.
There is a layer of liquid on top of my starter.	Usually, the liquid is safe. It is either excess water in the starter mixture or fermentation product that is often called 'hooch'. Hooch is a slightly alcoholic, acid water that is produced through long fermentation, or from a very active and vigorous fermentation. If it is hooch the aroma will be your best clue. If you have added too much water during a refresh the excess water will settle on the top of the starter within a few hours. If the starter is not refreshed and allowed to continue to ferment, eventually the fermenting flour will rise through the liquid layer and three reasonably distinct layers will form: the lower layer is fermenting flour. The middle layer is hooch and the upper layer is a bubbly mess of fermented flour. Eventually, the top layer will sink and return to the two layers: hooch on top, fermented flour below. Retaining hooch will increase the acidic or sour notes of the starter and any bread made using it. Removing hooch will slightly reduce the acidity and sour notes of the bread made with it.	In either situation, the simplest approach is to ignore the problem. There are two interventions that work well: 1. Remove the excess liquid by pouring it out. 2. Stir the excess liquid into the starter, then refresh as usual.
I left it in the fridge and I think I have killed it.	Eventually, a starter that is not cared for will appear to die. Some of the microbes will die. Some will shut down until conditions are right for them to get on with life. It is possible to revive a neglected starter; however, it can take almost as long as preparing a new starter culture. The population of microbes may or may not be similar to what it was. Some microbes may have suffered too much to recover to their previous numbers and vigour. Some microbes may find that reduced competition allows them to flourish.	Try reviving the starter, knowing that it is unlikely to be the same as it was. Or Prepare a new starter culture. Consider preparing your starter for storage if you know that you will not be using it for prolonged periods. See page 31.
I left it out on the bench when I was away, and now it is growing stuff.	See above: 'It has something growing on it.'	Unless you are able to identify all the microbes and confirm that they are safe, the best action is to dispose of the starter and prepare a new culture. When you begin a new culture ensure that all your implements and containers are clean and sterile.

Troubleshooting issues with sourdough starter:

What could possibly go wrong with sourdough starter?

Here are a few things:

My starter is very sour, I want to have a less sour starter.	Some starters are more sour than others. Buckwheat sourdough starters are, perhaps, the most sour of the gluten-free sourdough starters. The way we manage and maintain our starters will influence the acidity of the starter. More frequent refreshing at lower temperatures will prevent the starter from becoming too acidic and sour. If a starter is stored in the refrigerator, remove the start at least once a week to refresh it.	For a less sour starter choose quinoa or teff. To reduce the acidity of a starter take a small amount of the starter and refresh it in a clean, sterile container with a refresh ration of 1:2:2 (starter: flour: water). Refresh at least twice each day for 2 days.

Troubleshooting issues with dough:

What could possibly go wrong with dough?

Here are a few things:

Concern	Possible cause & explanation	Action
No obvious signs of fermentation.	Some doughs are slow to show signs of fermentation, especially in the early hours. That is normal. During the early stages of fermentation, enzymes are at work breaking down starches into sugars that are used by yeasts and bacteria. Initially, the yeasts and bacteria need to multiply. Eventually with the enzymes at work and the yeasts and bacteria populations increasing the dough will show signs of fermenting. The most obvious sign will be a visible expansion of the dough. If the starter is active it can take about 18 to 20 hours at room temperature for a dough made with 300g flour, 12g psyllium husk, and 3g salt, at 100% hydration with 20g of starter to be ready for baking. Most of that time is required for fermentation.	**Don't panic.** It may take a while. If the dough is a high yeast dough (more than 6g of yeast in 300g of flour), check that you included the yeast. If you are convinced that you did include the yeast, check the viability of the yeast by taking a few grams and mixing it in half a cup of warm water. If it is OK you should see bubbles form within 5 minutes.
The dough has no strength, its more like a thick slurry.	Look at the flour first. Is the flour fine or is it gritty? If it is gritty the problem is that there is little starch damage and the starch is not absorbing water. If the flour is fine, there may be too much water in the dough. Did you measure accurately?	Keep working and mixing the dough (you may want to use a mechanical mixer if you have one). This will help the water to penetrate the flour grains and eventually the starch granules will begin to absorb moisture.
The dough doesn't rise.	Structure of the dough is too open due to using a coarse flour. Consequently, gases are escaping through the dough.	Check the coarseness or fineness of the flour. If the flour is coarse it can be soaked before the dough is built. To do this take a large portion of the flour (up to 75%) and about 50% of the water and allow it to soak for at least 1 hour before mixing the dough. Adding a small amount of fat to the dough will assist to hold gasses in the dough. Olive oil or sunflower oil each work well in this way. The oil should be no more than 5% of the flour weight. If the formula already contains fat (butter or oil) this method will not resolve the issue.

Troubleshooting issues with the crust:

What could possibly go wrong with the crust?

Here are a few things:

Concern	Possible cause & explanation	Action
The crust is white. How do I get those lovely tan and brown colours?	A crust browns through two separate processes: the Maillard reaction, and caramelization. In the Maillard reaction compounds produced in the reaction are similar to those produced in toasting bread. Caramelization depends on water and sugars being present. Some ovens do not hold steam well. As the oven environment dries the surface of the crust may dry before caramelization takes place. If the oven is cooler than needed there may not be enough heat to initiate Maillard reactions.	Check the oven temperature using an oven thermometer to ensure that it is baking at the right temperature for the bread being baked. Conserve steam around the dough by covering the dough with a cloche, a deep baking pan or aluminium foil. Add steam to the environment during the initial stages of baking. [A little honey (between 2% and 5%) added to the dough can change a pale loaf to a glowing, well-tanned specimen!]
The crust tears in all sorts of places.	During baking, the dough expands (oven spring). At the same time, the crust is gelatinizing and drying out. The expanding dough needs somewhere to go. Weak spots in the skin of the dough tear.	Score the top of the loaf to control the places and the extent of tearing. Scoring patterns can serve a decorative function as well as the practical function of controlling the way a loaf expands. See page 40.
The crust is too dark.	A dark crust usually indicates that the loaf has been baked too hot, and or, there is plenty of sugar in the dough.	Check the oven temperature using an oven thermometer to ensure that it is baking at the right temperature for the bread being baked. Reduce the baking temperature and increase the baking time. To manage the colour of the crust. It may take a few bakes to produce the desired colour.
The crust is too tough and dry.	A tough dry crust indicates the loaf has been baked at too high a temperature for too long.	Check the oven temperature using an oven thermometer to ensure that it is baking at the right temperature for the bread being baked.

Troubleshooting issues with the crumb:

What could possibly go wrong with the crumb?

Here are a few things:

Concern	Possible cause & explanation	Action
The crumb is gummy.	What was the total time the dough was fermented? Gumminess can be due to the dough being over proved, or over fermented.	Allow the gummy loaf to rest for a day on a rack on the bench. This will allow some of the excess moisture to dry from the loaf.
	How long was it baked, and at what temperatures?	Be careful to measure accurately.
	Dough made with 300g flour, 12g psyllium husk, and 3g salt, at 100% hydration with 20g of starter usually needs about 60 minutes baking time at 200°C.	Recognize that each substitution has implications. Make detailed notes when substitutions are made. The notes may help identify the cause of undesirable outcomes.
	Is the oven baking at the indicated temperature?	
	Were the ingredients measured accurately?	Consider reducing the overall time allowed for fermentation.
	A few grams difference here or there can be accommodated by most of the formulas in this book. However, too many differences in the same dough may combine to create a problem.	
	Were any flours or other ingredients in the formula changed?	
	We need to consider the total formula. Any changes that are made may upset the balance and have an undesirable effect on the crumb.	
The crumb has a band of dense gooey dough near the bottom of the loaf.	What was the total time the dough was fermented? Gumminess can be due to the dough being over proved, or over fermented.	Reduce the total fermentation time.
		Reduce the temperature of fermentation.
	When we consider the baking temperature and the baking time, the aim is to get the temperature high enough for long enough so that the starches in the dough first gelatinize and then set.	
	Over fermenting the dough can reduce the strength of the crumb	
	So, it's not just a case of getting the dough up to the 96°C to 99°C range, we need to hold it there long enough for the dough to set. The challenge is to manage the bake time and temperature. Unfortunately, if the dough has not had time to set the structure will not be strong enough to hold the lovely bubbly shape.	
The crumb isn't there, it's just a big hole with a mass of goo in the bottom.	Oh dear! You have an extreme 'flying crust' or might call it a lava cave or a limestone cave.	Reduce the total fermentation time.
		Reduce the temperature of fermentation.
	In the section about gelatinization on page 47, the process of baking is discussed. The skin of the dough gelatinizes first, forming the crust. The crust then contains all the gases and the expanding dough, unless the expansion tears the crust. As heat flows through the dough the heat should gelatinize the starches in the dough unless fermentation has gone too far and there is insufficient starch left to provide structure to the gelatinizing dough. The gelatinized dough becomes gummy. Until the increase in temperature causes enzyme activity to slow down, the dough begins to mash transforming starches into sugars. This is similar to the process that is used to make malt syrup (see page 43).	

Bibliography

Audio recordings

History of millets:
https://www.npr.org/sections/thesalt/2015/12/23/460559052/millet-how-a-trendy-ancient-grain-turned-nomads-into-farmers (accessed April 22, 2019)

History of bread:
https://www.bbc.co.uk/sounds/play/b09vz6r3 (accessed April 22, 2019)

Technical papers
Malting buckwheat

Wijngaard, H.H. and Arendt, E.K. 'Optimisation of a Mashing Program for 100% Malted Buckwheat.' *J. Inst. Brew.* 112(1), 57–65, 2006

Books
Bertinet, Richard. *Crumb – show the dough who's boss.* London: Kyle Books, 2019.

Buehler, Emily. *Bread Science – the chemistry and craft of making bread.* Hillsborough: Two Blue Books, 2006.

Calvel, Raymond, Ronald L. Writs, James J. MacGuire. *The Taste of Bread.* New York: Springer Science+Business Media, 2001.

Fromartz, Samuel. *In Search of the Perfect Loaf – A home baker's odyssey.* New York: Viking, 2014.

Hadjiandreou, Emmanuel. *How to Make Sourdough – 45 recipes for great-tasting sourdough breads that are good for you too.* London: Ryland Peters & Small, 2016.

Halliday, David. *The Bloody History of the Croissant.* North Melbourne: Arcadia, 2010.

Hamelman, Jeffrey. *Bread – A baker's book of techniques and recipes.* New Jersey: Wiley, 2013.

Hedh, Jan. *Artisan Breads – Practical recipes and detailed instructions for baking the world's finest loaves.* New York: Skyhorse Publishing, 2004.

James, Michael; James, Pippa. *The Tivoli Road Baker – Breads - Pastries - Doughnuts - Pies - Cakes.* Melbourne: Hardie Grant Books, 2017.

Kimbell, Vanessa. *The Sourdough School – The ground-breaking guide to making gut-friendly bread.* London: Kyle Books, 2018.

Lepard, Dan. *The Handmade Loaf.* London: Mitchell Beasley, 2004.

Nosrat, Samir. *Salt Fat Acid Heat – Mastering the elements of good cooking.* New York: Simon & Schuster, 2017.

Whitley, Andrew. *Bread Matters – Why and how to make your own.* London: 4th Estate, 2009.

Young, Chris; and the bakers of the Real Bread Campaign. *Slow Dough – Real Bread.* London: Nourish, 2016.

Glossary

Amaranth: a short-lived perennial plant of the *Amaranthaceae* family, from Central America. It is cultivated as leaf vegetables, pseudocereal seeds and ornamental use. The seed is high in amino acids (hence high in proteins). It should be used freshly milled.

Acetic acid: produced by heterofermentative lactic acid bacteria during sourdough fermentation, particularly at lower temperatures.

Alveoli (alveolus): small air cavities or bubbles in the starter, and in the dough that open the structure of the dough.

Arborio rice: short grain rice from northern Italy, now grown around the world. Arborio rice has a higher level of amylopectin starch. It is very useful milled as a flour for making softer rice-based bread.

Autolysis or autolyse: a technique that improves hydration of the flour and allows the enzymes to begin transforming the flour before leaven is added to the dough. This technique was described by Raymond Calvel. *The Taste of Bread*, Springer Science+Business Media, New York, 2001.

Banneton: a proving basket designed to hold the shape of a formed lump of dough as it undergoes its final ferment before baking. A banneton is designed to permit the dough skin, that will become the crust of the loaf, to lose some moisture, thus firming compared to the inner dough.

Bassinage: a technique that improves hydration of the flour by withholding about 10% of the water from the main dough, then adding it after a rest of about 30 minutes. This allows more water to be worked into the dough and assists in promoting damage of starches in the dough to enhance hydration.

Binder: gums such as xanthan gum, guar gum are often called binders as they help to hold gluten-free doughs together. Sometimes psyllium husk is also called a binder.

Buckwheat: an annual plant of the *Polygonaceae* family native to Eurasia. The seeds are rich in complex carbohydrates and, like some other gluten-free seeds are referred to as a pseudocereal. Buckwheat seeds mill easily to produce fine flour. Fermented buckwheat contains hydrocolloids that assist in providing structure to dough.

Chia: the seed of the annual plant *Salvia hispanica*, from central and southern Mexico. The seed is nutrient rich and, when wetted, produces a hydrocolloid gel that can be used to assist in forming a dough matrix.

Crumb: the inner part of the bread, not the crust.

Diastatic malt: a flour produced by germinating seed, then arresting germination to take advantage of the increased levels of enzymes generated during seed germination.

Dough matrix: the structure of dough that enables alveoli or gas bubbles to form. In gluten-free bread, the formation of a dough matrix depends on fine flour and damaged starch granules as well as other fine particles and fats (naturally present in wholegrain flour, or other added fats), along with a hydrocolloid of some type.

Dough temperature: the internal temperature of the dough. The dough temperature can be modified by heating or cooling, or by mixing the dough with pre-heated or pre-cooled ingredients. In this book, most doughs are made, fermented and proved at room temperature. Some, like croissants, use chilled ingredients, others use tepid water to increase the initial dough temperature. A few doughs are made with very hot or boiling water to pre-gelatinize part of the dough before mixing.

Enriched dough: dough that includes added sugar, milk, fats and eggs to modify the dough and enrich the texture and flavours of the final bread. See formulas for enriched bread on pages 155 to 187.

Exopolysaccharide (EPS): a polysaccharide secreted by microorganisms outside of their cell membrane. In seed germination, EPS form a protective biofilm. In breadmaking, EPS enhance the dough matrix.

Fermentation temperature: most doughs in this book are fermented at room temperature (around 20 degrees Celsius). Some doughs are fermented at lower temperatures to extend the fermentation time and modify the fermentation processes performed by some of the lactic acid bacteria.

Flax: the seed of the annual plant *Linnum usitatissimum*, from the Caucasus region of Eurasia. The seed is nutrient rich and, when wetted, produces a hydrocolloid gel that can be used to assist in forming a dough matrix. The fibres of the flax plant are used to make linen that the traditional cloth used in a baker's couche.

Glycaemic index: is the relative ranking of the carbohydrates available in foods. Carbohydrates in foods classes ranked at 55 or below are more slowly digested, absorbed and metabolised. Carbohydrates in foods classes ranked at 70 or above are more rapidly digested, absorbed and metabolised.

Guar gum: gum derived from the bean seed of *Cyamopsis tetragonoloba*. The gum is a polysaccharide that can be used as a dough improver.

Gum: a substance that is largely composed of polysaccharides, and/or oligosaccharides. When mixed with water it forms a hydrocolloid that can be used to enhance the dough matrix.

Hydration: the process of wetting starch granules and other components of dough so that water is absorbed and held in molecular bonds.

Hydrocolloid: a gel-like substance formed by hydration of polysaccharides, and/or oligosaccharides. Hydrocolloids are important components of the dough matrix.

Knead: to mix wet and dry ingredients of dough together with the intention of forming a consistent dough matrix. Ingredients can be mixed by hand, with tools, or by machine.

Lactic acid: an acid produced by lactic acid bacteria, lactic acid confers a mild sour flavour to the dough, it also improves the texture of dough and other sensory qualities, as well as shelf life.

Lactic acid bacteria (LAB): a group of bacteria that produce lactic acid as waste material. LAB are classified as:

- homofermentative – bacteria that produce a single end product
- heterofermentative – bacteria that produce more than one product
- facultative – bacteria that produce more than one product, where the product depends on the environmental conditions at the time.

Lamination: the process of encapsulating solid fats (usually butter) into a folded dough. When baked the laminated dough opens into many light layers. In this book, techniques for lamination are described in formulas for Wholegrain Croissants (page 181), Buckwheat Croissants (page 183), and Brioche Feuiettée (page 187).

Lean dough: a basic dough consisting of flour (plus hydrocolloid in gluten-free dough), salt, and water, with no enriching ingredients.

Leaven: a substance use for raising dough. For most of human history, the leaven is a natural ferment either intentionally added, or cultured as part of the bread making process. In more recent times selected strains of yeast, as well as chemical substances (like bicarbonate of soda) have been used to raise dough.

Lievito madre: low hydration, or 'stiff' dough developed as a leaven for preparing light and delicate doughs. Usually, a naturally fermented yeast product prepared in an Italian tradition. It is a stiff sourdough starter. Lievito is yeast, madre is mother. Some bakers use the name interchangeably with pasta (dough) madre. The 'mother' indicates the original yeast source that provides life again and again and again to bread. The mother, fed, refreshed, and cared for with great diligence continues to provide the life to a range of breads, for many years.

Maillard reaction: a chemical reaction that depends on heat, sugar, amino acids, and amines. Carbohydrates and proteins are degraded through heat. Many combinations of flavour and colour compounds are formed. Exactly which ones are formed depends on the temperature, acidity, chemicals available.

Malt: a flour or powder developed from germinated seed to take advantage of the higher enzyme activity available through germination. Germination is arrested by drying the seed. The rootlets are mechanically removed from the dried seed and the seed is either milled (for diastatic malt flour) or toasted then milled for malt powders that are used for colouring and flavouring.

Malting: the process of preparing malt products. See pages 42 & 43.

Millet: a grass of the *Poaceae* family. In various formulas in this book, the following millets are used: proso millet, sorghum, and teff.

Mother: a dough culture prepared a from flour and water. The mother is the source of yeast and bacteria used to inoculate bread dough to promote fermentation. The mother is fed, refreshed, and cared for with great diligence so that it will continue to provide the life to a range of breads for many years.

Oligosaccharide: branched, short chain polymers containing a small number (typically less than 10) of simple sugars.

Oven spring: the expansion of bread dough during the early stages of baking.

Pasta madre: see Lievito madre

Phytate: a stored form of phosphorus, bound to other minerals, found in outer layers of seeds and usually concentrated in the bran. During hydration and fermentation, the strong molecular bonds of phytates are weakened and the minerals become more available as nutrients.

Polysaccharide: long chain, and branched polymers containing a large number (typically more than 10) of simple sugars. During fermentation, polysaccharides are often broken down to simpler forms of sugars and other products during fermentation.

Prove (Proof): the final stage of fermentation of dough before baking.

Proving basket: a container used to hold dough during the final stage of fermentation. A proving basket, or banneton, is designed to draw moisture from the skin of the dough that will form the crust of the loaf. A proving basket can be improvised from a clean cloth and a bowl, or other rigid, or semi-rigid, container.

Psyllium husk: the seed husk of the *Plantago* genus that is rich in hydrocolloids useful for enhancing the dough matrix.

Quinoa: an annual plant of the *Chenopodium* genus,

originating in Peru. Quinoa is grown for its nutrient-rich seed. The seed, when cleaned to remove the protective saponin coating, is easily milled to a fine flour.

Room temperature: usually considered to be about 20 degrees Celsius.

Scalding: a technique that improves hydration of the flour and changes the structure of starches in the flour by mixing a portion of the flour with boiling water. When the flour is scalded the starches are rapidly gelatinized.

Sourdough: a natural ferment cultured from a mixture of flour and water.

Sorghum: a grass from the millet family.

Starter: a cultured, ferment of water and flour used to initiate fermentation in bread dough.

Sweet rice (sticky rice, glutinous rice): varieties of rice that have high ratios of the starch amylopectin, relative to the starch amylose.

Tangzhong roux: a mixture of flour and water (typically 1 part flour to 5 parts water) that is cooked to initiate gelatinization of the starches in the flour.

Teff: a grass from the millet family.

Vinegar: a product of the fermentation plant materials (usually fruit or seeds) that is high in acetic acid.

Wholegrain (whole seed): the complete grain, or seed, usually excluding the seed husk. Wholegrain flour contains all the components of the whole seed.

Xanthan gum: an exopolysaccharide produced by fermentation of a carbohydrate-rich substrate by the bacterium *Xanthomonas campestris*.

Yeast: single-celled fungi that abound in nature. In bread baking, selected strains of the yeast *Saccharomyces cerevisiae* have been commonly used for over 100 years. In nature, there are over 1500 identified yeasts. Some yeasts are toxic to humans or produce toxic products. In natural ferments, so-called 'wild yeasts' are harnessed, along with lactic acid bacteria and other bacteria to ferment bread dough.

Yeast water: a natural ferment usually based on fruits, sugars, and/or honey that contains a range of yeasts and bacteria used for fermenting bread dough. Where in sourdough the balance of microbes favours lactic acid bacteria, in yeast waters the sugar-rich environment is designed to favour yeasts.

Index

CPSIA information can be obtained
at www.ICGtesting.com
Printed in the USA
LVHW070855080720
660059LV00027B/430